Parenting from the Heart

A Guide to the Essence of Parenting from the Inside-Out

Jack Pransky, Ph.D.
© 1997; 2012

CCB Publishing
British Columbia, Canada

Parenting from the Heart:
A Guide to the Essence of Parenting from the Inside-Out

Copyright © 1997; 2012 by Jack Pransky
ISBN-13 978-1-927360-64-4
Fourth Edition

Library and Archives Canada Cataloguing in Publication
Pransky, Jack, 1946-
Parenting from the heart : a guide to the essence of parenting from the inside-
out / written by Jack Pransky – 4th ed.
Includes bibliographical references.
ISBN 978-1-927360-64-4
Also available in electronic format.
1. Parenting. 2. Parent and child. 3. Child rearing. I. Title.
HQ755.8.P72 2012   649'.1   C2012-903862-8

Initial Editing by Martha Gagliardi
Illustrations by Shirley H. Pransky
Cover drawing by Jaime E. Pransky (at age 15)

To order *Parenting from the Heart* and Jack Pransky's other books:
Copies may be ordered from the publisher, any bookstore, Amazon.com or
the Center for Inside-Out Understanding, jack@healthrealize.com,
310 Dickerson, Rd., Moretown, VT 05660 ~ Tel: (802) 249-0620.
Quantity discounts are available. For information on lectures, seminars,
workshops or trainings with Jack Pransky, see www.healthrealize.com or
call (802) 249-0620.

Publisher: CCB Publishing, British Columbia, Canada
               www.ccbpublishing.com

To the lights of my life—my wonderful children:
David and Jaime

ACKNOWLEDGEMENTS

Very special thanks to Dr. George Pransky, without whose insights this book initially never would have been written.

And to Jaime, David and Judy for their contributions, and for my life during that time.

And in memoriam to ~

Dr. H. Stephen Glenn for helping me to be a far more effective parent.

Dr. Roger Mills, and to Sydney Banks, without whose insights George Pransky and Roger Mills and I would likely not have had our insights.

Russell Smith for his early book production work.

Shirley Pransky, my mother, for providing the illustrations, and to both my parents for raising me so well.

FOREWORD

For over thirty years I studied issues involved in raising children and preparing them for the challenges of life. During this time I conducted thousands of workshops, seminars and courses for parents, foster parents, step-parents and educators. Through this experience it has become increasingly apparent that the majority of people faced with the challenges of child rearing often look to "experts" for direction, techniques and "the answers" to the endless questions that arise in working with children.

While it is always appropriate to seek *wisdom*, it is also true that every relationship is a unique synthesis of dynamic and constantly changing variables in which *inspiration* is often as important as knowledge. The challenge of balancing heart and head is like an endless walk down a tightrope in which knowledge helps us know what needs to be done and the heart provides the balance necessary to do it under the pressures of each moment. Learning to live in and trust our *inner light* is particularly difficult for those of us raised in the western world.

In *Parenting from the Heart* Jack Pransky offers practical wisdom grounded in intimate experiences with his own children. Most clearly, the message of being open and respectful comes through in the emphasis on collaborative problem solving and family management. In an era in which media often overwhelms us with the weird, the bazaar, the negative and often the frightening aspects of human health and behavior, it is refreshing to celebrate with Jack the innate goodness and potential for healthy living that lies within humanity. To see these qualities within children and nurture them in body, mind and spirit so that health can be realized and expressed as spontaneous element of life is one of the greatest contributions one generation can make to the next.

While the rate and intensity with which knowledge, technology and lifestyle are changing has created a world without reliable maps or guideposts, the compass of a clear mind and an open heart provides unique direction and light within the chaos. The wise and practical steps offered in this book provide comfort and support for those of us who are open to raising children as a process in which our children are also teachers and fellow travelers.

Over the years I have become increasingly concerned over the number of books and courses on childrearing that are prescriptive in nature and that offer "the way" to deal with various issues that are inevitable in working with children. It has been my experience that every child is a unique person and every relationship is unique and constantly changing. Therefore, an appropriate response to a given issue with a given child at a given moment in time may be totally inappropriate for that same child (let alone another) under different circumstances.

While most people seek the security of a cookbook, anyone who has tried to use one knows sooner or later you end up changing a recipe to reflect your own needs and tastes. On this important issue Jack Pransky takes the high road and offers support and a guide for those with the courage to live and grow in the process of life-touching-life. He resists the temptation to rescue us by offering *his solutions* and, instead, models the principles this book advocates by encouraging us to discover *our own*. Perhaps it should be said that *this book is not for the faint-of-heart!*

- H. Stephen Glenn
Author, Raising Self-Reliant Children in a Self-Indulgent World
and the parenting course,
Developing Capable People

PREFACE TO THE FOURTH EDITION

This book has been the best kept secret in parenting.

This is not really something to be proud of, not so much for myself as author but for the thousands or millions more parents who would benefit.

I know this because parents who have read earlier editions of *Parenting from the Heart* have told me as much. Since it first came out in 1997 this book has touched many lives over those years. It has helped many parents create beautiful relationships with their children, even when things had become so bad they didn't think it even possible. It has helped many children's lives blossom and grow well into adulthood.

When a parent writes, "This book saved my life and it probably saved my children's lives too," nothing can be more gratifying for an author to hear.

Yet so many parents are still in need! If the truth be known I have never cared much about marketing (of myself especially). I do care that ever-increasing numbers of children are raised in the healthiest way possible for the benefit of themselves, their parents and future society.

Looking back since I first wrote this book it is easy for me to see how my understanding of what creates people's experience of life and what makes them function as they do has deepened considerably. Yet, the foundation of what is needed to raise children in the healthiest way remains. Therefore I wanted this edition of the book to remain essentially the same but be updated to reflect my own deeper understanding.

This approach to parenting is very different from what people will find in nearly all parenting courses and other parenting books. Don't get me wrong, parenting courses and other approaches have been helpful for many people, but I see now when they have to point people to techniques and skills they are off the essence. The essence of parenting means pointing people inside themselves to their own wisdom, which they can draw upon in any situation, making it so much more helpful. Every parent knows naturally, deep within themselves, the healthiest way to raise their children and to know how to deal with any discipline issues or problem behavior that arise—if they know what this innate wisdom is, how it gets there, what keeps it obscured, and how to access it.

I hope skilled practitioners with this inside-out understanding will take what is offered here and create parenting groups and classes, or use one-on-one as appropriate, to spread this message around to reach as many parents as possible.

Or, the beauty of this book is that it can be devoured and used in the privacy of one's own home to create healthy, joyful relationships, one family at a time.

No matter what, I can almost guarantee that this approach to parenting, if taken to heart and put into practice, will improve relationships between parents and their children and will bring out the best in both.

Jack Pransky
Moretown, Vermont
March, 2012

PREFACE TO THE FIRST EDITION

This is not the book it started to be.

For ten years I had run many parenting courses and trained many parenting course instructors. For my book, *Prevention: The Critical Need*, I had thoroughly researched every known theory on parenting that I could find. I believed I knew most everything one could know about the subject. In my own home I had successfully put into practice what I had learned. I intended to write a book called, "The Pocket Encyclopedia of Parenting and Discipline" that would cut through to the essentials of all known parenting theories and techniques, list problem situations parents most often encounter with their children and offer solutions based on those theories and techniques.

I then stumbled upon a new approach that caused me to question everything I thought I knew. This shocked me, for this new approach had emerged not from any parenting theory but from what could be called a "new" understanding of how the human mind functions to cause people (parents and children included) to feel and behave as they do [which has since come to be called, "The Three Principles," a.k.a. "Health Realization," "Innate Health" or "State of Mind Training"]

Previously I had been saying, "Parenting is the toughest job any of us can do." Yet, this new approach made parenting seem comparatively so effortless and joyful. The way I had been trained, there always seemed to be so much to remember and do. Despite my knowledge and skills even I found it difficult to always stay on top of the right technique to use in a given situation, especially when I was upset or frustrated.

I am not at all suggesting that what I had learned previously was a bad idea or a waste of time; on the contrary, it helped me develop a good relationship with my own children. However, when I decided to test out this new approach on my family, low and behold, our relationships markedly improved—and it seemed so much easier! At first I thought this approach too simple. But it worked! The reason? It pointed me within. It told me to put aside all the techniques I had learned and, instead, tuned me into what my heart told me to do.

While Dr. George Pransky had developed a set of tapes on this approach—and I highly recommend it [if it is still available—see Bibliography]—when I began writing this no book about applying this approach to parenting had yet been written.* I set aside my "Pocket Encyclopedia," for I knew in my heart that this new approach was right and would be far more valuable.

I have found this to be the happiest and most productive way to deal with children and teenagers. Enjoy!

Jack Pransky
Cabot, Vermont
September, 1997

---

*Note: Later, Dr. Roger Mills (1995) published the *Health Realization Parent Manual* [now out of print].

CONTENTS

INTRODUCTION

No set of discipline techniques will give you a good relationship with your children.

Discipline techniques are only fine-tuning mechanisms. As on a television set the fine-tuning knob will only work when the signal is strong enough. The feeling is the signal. The feeling is what we feel in our hearts and the relationships we build. If the right feeling is not present discipline will not work. At best we will get begrudging, temporary compliance.

This book goes beyond techniques to the feeling.

In essence, two understandings lie at the heart of parenting:

1. Our children always carry within them all the well-being, wisdom and common sense that they will ever need; it only needs to be drawn out and nurtured in the kind of loving environment that will help it flourish.

2. Our children can access this innate health and wisdom by understanding that they have it, discovering where it comes from, seeing how they think in ways that keep them from realizing it and recognizing that it appears most when their minds are calm or clear.

Then they can let it guide their lives.

The same is true for parents. We can access this health and well-being at any time to guide our parenting.

As trees in a forest naturally gravitate toward the light, when we create the kind of environment that draws out this natural health and wisdom we naturally guide our children in healthy ways and away from unproductive feelings and disruptive behaviors.

In a nutshell that is what this book is about.

1

I. LIVING IN AN ENVIRONMENT OF LOVE AND POSITIVE FEELINGS

"You don't understand kids!" my then fifteen year-old daughter kept telling me.

This puzzled me.

Me, not understand kids? Me?! Had I not devoted my entire life to preventing problems among young people and even wrote a book about it? Had I not run many parenting courses and trained many parenting instructors? Most important, did I not have what I considered to be a good relationship with my own daughter?

"Jaime, what do you mean by that?" I asked.

"You just don't."

Not overly helpful! But I did want to understand. My daughter could not articulate it. She had only a vague feeling.

I did see Jaime taking less and less responsibility for herself. If anything went wrong she would always blame someone or something else. She always had an excuse. She began to treat her mother with contempt. We also saw Jaime becoming increasingly unhappy. This concerned us deeply, for we seemed powerless to do anything about it.

Then, one day, Jaime had a breakthrough. She had been too close to see it.

It began the night she stayed over at a friend's house, after her friend had attended a huge party and had not bothered to inform her parents. Jaime watched the mother confront her friend about misrepresenting her whereabouts and not coming home when expected. The mother said they had given her a certain amount of trust and freedom; it was a big deal to let a fourteen-year-old go to a party and she should have shown her parents more respect.

Jaime watched her friend completely shut her mother out, not listen to anything she said. Jaime could relate. Her

3

friend had heard her mother say such things a hundred times and it had stopped registering. Instead of taking in its truth her friend got snotty and angry and yelled, "You don't understand anything!"

It looked all too familiar. Observing it from a distance, not caught up in the emotions, not feeling threatened Jaime realized that she too had a tendency to react in the same way whenever a power figure loomed over her. To Jaime, her friend's mother made a lot of sense. *Trust* was at stake! Her friend's parents needed to know what her friend was up to. How else would they know whether to stay up until she had arrived home safely, or if she had stayed over at someone's house, or if she'd been raped and was lying somewhere in a gutter.

Jaime could relate to the feeling. Whenever her own parents got on her case about anything, rather than listen her mind would be scrambling trying to figure out what she could say to protect herself, blocking out the words, saying over and over to herself, "This is so stupid! This is so stupid!"

Jaime thought, "It must be something about the way all parents come across: 'This-is-the-way-it's-going-to-be-and-if-it's-not-here's-what-will-happen.' But in the end kids make their own decisions anyway, no matter what their parents say."

The next day, at our own house, Jaime's mother, Judy, came in exhausted from a hard day's work to find that Jaime had a lot of friends over and had basically trashed the house.

"Jaime, I can't believe you could do this!" Judy snapped.

Jaime felt herself tuning out from her mother as her friend had. She could pick up the slightest edge in a tone of voice miles away—long before her mother even noticed it in herself. Jaime's antennae were way up. She would be waiting to pounce whenever she heard a tone change,

4

which invariably resulted in the butting of heads and a fight.

No one veered from their positions. In the middle of the argument it occurred to Judy that they were having a power struggle; that Jaime was trying to assert her power and Judy's own power was holding it back. She attempted to express this to Jaime, but Jaime didn't hear it as intended.

So frustrated and red-faced it looked like she would burst, Jaime yelled, "I hate you! I hate you! I love you because you're my mother, but I hate you!"

Judy was at wit's end.

"It's not like it was!" Jaime cried. "You don't hold me anymore and tell me you love me like you used to. You're just on my case. You just come in and say how disappointed you are in me, how I let you down. I can't live up to your expectations of me!"

"What do you want me to do?" Judy replied. "Is it too much to expect you not to add to my burden when I come home?"

At this point Jaime grabbed her head and let out a scream. "AAAUUUGHHH! I can't stand it anymore!"

I was sitting on the other side of the room watching all this. (I do not mean to suggest that I came riding in on a white horse here; Judy had bailed me out on many an occasion.) However, as I was not personally involved in the conversation—as detached as Jaime had been with her friend—I was not the one feeling threatened, causing my guard to be up. So while Judy saw this as an issue of power, I heard something else.

"Wait," I said, "the point isn't power. The point is love. Jaime is saying that we could tell her to do anything, so long as we say it with love and understanding."

Jaime nodded through her tears. No matter what we told her it could be communicated in a nonaccusatory way—in a loving way. I realized if love isn't being felt in the moment, only then do issues of power come into play.

Judy then had a breakthrough. "Oh, you mean it's not what I say, it's how I say it?"

We could say, "Jaime, honey, would you mind picking this up please," instead of, "How could you do this!" and have her take it as a personal affront.

Jaime said, "Even when you're mad—especially around little things, like if you leave your light on, it should be, like, 'Jaime, honey, you left your light on,' or saying it with a smile on your face. Things get across to kids better that way. Because it doesn't really matter in the whole scheme of things. It can bug you, but it can bug you in a happy way, as opposed to, 'Why don't you ever do that right!'"

My God, she is right! She is so right!

It's the key to it all.

I was even writing about it and I didn't see it under my nose. I understood it on an intellectual level but it had not connected in my heart. Of course I knew this, but knowing it intellectually means nothing.

Our daughter helped us see that this is the only thing that really counts in parenting. It's the cake; everything else is the icing. *What our kids feel from us in the moment is the only thing that really matters.*

This goes for our own kids, as well as any kids we work with or teach.

It must go beyond intellectual understanding—to the heart.

We can see it in those who work best with kids; we can see it in the teachers that students love. Such individuals naturally create a loving, supportive, lighthearted feeling. Teenagers, children, feel it from them—even if they're tough and demand a lot. This is why they are so good with kids and help them have breakthroughs in understanding.

In a sense it does not even matter what we say. It's what our children feel coming out of us toward them from our hearts.

Every day I thank my lucky stars for this breakthrough. At ages sixteen and seventeen Jaime was an absolute delight to be around, to have around. We developed the most wonderful, warm, loving relationship. By her senior year people kept commenting to us about how happy and self-assured Jaime always seemed to be.

In sum, here is the essence of what is being said: If we want our children to both respond to us well and live a life of well-being, they must live in a loving feeling. The number one most-important-by-far-bar-none thing that we can do for our children is to *create a loving, supportive, caring, respectful, lighthearted environment* for our kids to thrive in. And we don't need to know any parenting techniques to do it.

Of course we know this! This is not new news. But there is one catch: A loving environment is a moment-to-moment thing.

What?

The feeling we have at the time is the environment the child is living in at that moment.

When we feel angry, our children are living in an angry environment. When we feel scared, our children are living in a fearful environment. When we feel disappointed our children are living in an environment of, "I-can't-live-up-to-their-expectations." No matter what we try to communicate to them at those times the feeling we have inside us is what they pick up, the environment that surrounds them at that moment. If we are fearful or anxious or worried or angry or disappointed or any number of emotions, our children are not living in a loving, caring, supportive, environment at those times—even if we generally show love to our children and tell them many times a day that we love them. If we think they are, we're kidding ourselves.

LOVE IN THE MOMENT

So what does this suggest we do?

Another story may help illustrate this. A few years before I realized all this I was listening to a tape about relationships based on this same inside-out approach, called "Can Love Survive Commitment" by Darlene and

Charles Stewart. Toward the end of the tape Darlene began to describe the very difficult time they had been having with their teenage son who was getting into a lot of trouble. She said they had been trying to change him, trying to get him to do what was right—to no avail. One day it struck her. She said to herself [something like], "I decided I was going to stop trying to change him, I was just going to love him—even if I have to bring him cookies in jail."

The "cookies in jail" line got to me. It struck me as a completely wild, profound idea.

Darlene decided to back off trying to make him right. She simply went out of her way to show him love. Their relationship improved enormously. Remarkably, her son's troubling behaviors began to diminish.

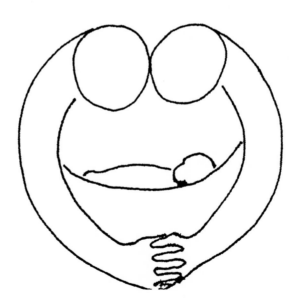

Despite how it affected me at the time I heard it and how it had helped me at the time to deal with my son, I had all but forgotten about it until this incident with my daughter. Now it came roaring back. I decided on the spot that I would commit to ignoring my thoughts of disappointment about what she was or wasn't doing right. Before I communicated anything to her I decided to watch what was in my heart to be sure I sent out love. I decided to go out of my way to create that loving environment around her at every moment I could, certainly every moment I wanted to communicate anything to her. Judy ended up doing the same.

It worked! We became much closer and, miraculously, Jaime became more helpful. When we backed off she responded.

The irony did not go unnoticed. The more we were on her case the less it worked. The less we were on her case the more it worked.

Everyone responds to love, respect, caring, support, lightheartedness. *Everyone responds when there is a good feeling in a relationship.*

II. INNATE HEALTH AND COMMON SENSE

In raising children, why would building a loving, caring, supportive, lighthearted atmosphere work?

To answer this we begin with an important point: *The way we see our children will determine how successful we will be in raising them.*

Read that again.

What we see is what we get.

If we see someone as lovable we tend to treat that person as lovable. When someone is treated in a lovable way that person tends to respond in a more lovable way. If we see someone as mean and rotten we tend to treat that person as if s/he is. People feel the way we treat them and respond accordingly.

Each of us has the opportunity to see our children in any way we want. We decide.

The way I have come to see children is to look deeply into their very nature. What I see is *within the spiritual essence of all children (and all other people) lies a pure state that yields natural mental health and well-being, and when this state or essence is allowed to flow freely from within unencumbered, children and others naturally behave in healthy ways.*

I don't want anyone to simply take my word for this. I would suggest your own observation. For example, take a close look at little babies. Until the "real world" starts impinging on their senses in a way that makes them feel uncomfortable, they are pure joy and pure wonder. Pure love. Pure innocence. A perfect little package. No insecure thoughts.

Think of the feeling you had in your heart the first time you saw your newborn. What most of us feel for that precious little infant in that moment is what they are naturally born with. This pure joy and wonder is part of their spirit. It's what makes them what they are. It exists apart from any physical infirmities they may bring with them into the world (including in their brains). It lies beyond all that. It is the human spirit, and that spirit is perfection. It is inside them and never goes away. Never—for any of us!

It certainly looks to me that the human spirit is always glowing inside people, even when it no longer appears like they have it. We may think it disappears given the way our kids behave sometimes, but the following three chapters will show why kids behave in problematic ways. For now all we need to know is, no matter what painful, difficult or traumatic experiences we go through, no matter what kinds of thoughts we develop about ourselves and others, no matter how much we forget we have it, we still have this natural, healthy state inside us, and we always have access to it, for it is the essence of who we are. So do our children.

We might be able to picture this innate health as the seed of a flower. The seed contains within it all the information it ever needs to grow into a healthy flower. All we have to do is put it in the right environment—the right moisture, sunlight, warmth, soil—and it will grow into a flower on its own. The seed is naturally "programmed" that way. It appears to me the same is true naturally in our children. Put children in a loving, warm, caring, nurturing, lighthearted environment and they will blossom and flourish, because it draws out what they already are within.

I am not suggesting little children do not have different temperaments or mental impairments or different chemicals within them that contribute to behavioral issues. Here I am talking about something far deeper than that: the human spirit itself and what it naturally brings them. I am suggesting this is the most helpful way to see our children.

MOVING TOWARD HEALTH

It would help us parents to recognize this essence in our kids. It would help us to see that each of our children (and this includes us because we were all children once) really *is* this natural state of pure spirit and therefore natural mental health, well-being, peace of mind, happiness, self-esteem and the ability to act with wisdom and common sense and to do what's best for themselves and others. It is a God-given, innate, completely natural state. We need only have faith and trust that it is there, no matter how our kids are behaving.

To see this would mean realizing that no child is born bad. Kids are healthier inside than we think. They have within them everything they need to have a happy, healthy life. Could we trust this in them?

How do we know this is true?

It cannot be proven.

Suppose some parents do not believe their children have innate health. What if it is too big a leap of faith? That's okay, but might those parents be able to accept that their children at least have the capability to act in healthy ways? If we look closely at people we might observe that even the most troubling or troubled people have moments when they act in healthier or more constructive ways than at other times. This means they have this capacity within them. And this capacity can be tapped or nurtured or brought out.

Yet suppose even that statement is too great a leap for some parents. For those parents who don't believe it, if they were simply to treat their children *as if* they had innate health or the capacity to attain it at any moment they could see for themselves whether it made a difference. My guess is they would be far better off because their children would feel it and respond accordingly.

Those who truly see the health in people can feel it. They know that all people, no matter how terribly they act in moments, have this inalienable spirit inside them. They know no one is born insecure or destructive or disruptive or inherently with bad thoughts of others; babies, children, adults have to learn and acquire these. They know when they see their children or anyone act out, it means that person is only lost; they've lost their bearings or their perspective. They have simply lost touch with the spiritual essence within them. *If our children become lost—and this seems to happen to all children from time to time—our job becomes to help them find themselves again. Our job is to help draw out their health.* No, we may not be able to prove the existence of inner spirit/innate health; all we know is those who have faith in it and treat their children and others as if they have these essential qualities usually get better results than those who do not.

In sum, for practical reasons if nothing else, even if we cannot find it in our hearts to accept that our children have innate health and wisdom, we can act toward them as if they do. Simply by seeing this we will find ourselves on the right path to productive and satisfying parenting.

For what we see is what we get.

DRAWING OUT HEALTH

This answers the question of why it works to establish a warm, loving, caring, lighthearted environment. Simply put, it draws out what is already inside. Like the trees in the forest that naturally gravitate toward the light, our children have a natural tendency to move toward their mental health and well-being, toward happiness, toward good feelings about themselves, toward peace of mind, toward healthy, productive relationships.

Children respond better in this kind of atmosphere because they gravitate to their true nature.

It would not be difficult to create this kind of climate if we could only carry around in our hearts every day the same beautiful feelings for our children that we experienced when they were first born, or when as little beings they had just done something exceptionally cute and endearing. It would be the most natural thing in the world.

Here are two pieces of good news:

1. That beautiful feeling for our children—carried in our hearts and communicated to them through our spirit—can overcome any lack of knowledge of specific parenting skills;

2. We already have that feeling for our children—it is already there. It is part of the perfect essence inside us.

The problem is when we're caught up in the emotions of the moment we forget. If our child has been defying us over time it can be especially hard to recapture that feeling. Yet, the initial, beautiful feeling never goes away—even when our kids are acting out or not doing what they should. This feeling is an inherent part of us. It may be buried or hidden or covered up but it is never gone.

How do we know this?

Did you ever notice that when you get upset or angry, once that upset or anger fades and the problem is resolved, the good feeling eventually comes back? Or, if a bad feeling has built over time (due to serious problems) every once in a while when your guard is down, or when your child's is down, you can feel that good feeling slip through even when you aren't expecting it, if only for a moment. And during that moment, if only fleeting, you glimpse the kind of relationship you want with your children. That we can experience it even for a moment means we have that capacity inside us. All we have to do is understand better how to find it and have it become our predominant feeling when dealing with our children.

SUMMARY

To summarize, if we really pay attention to what this means and listen to our own wisdom we realize a few things:

- Those warm, beautiful, loving feelings for our children are always there; they've just been covered up by extraneous thoughts.
- We can access those feelings—because from time to time we do.
- When we do, we have a nice relationship—even if it lasts only a short time.
- The more we access those warm feelings the better our relationship will be.

How can we find that warm, good feeling when we don't feel that feeling?

The odd thing is, to find it we do not need to do anything. Remember, we already have that feeling lying deep within our hearts, so all we have to do is get out of its way. We need to get out of our own way to allow what is naturally inside us to rise to the surface. *Only one thing can get in its way: our own thoughts. Our own thinking is the only thing that can keep us from feeling it.*

The next chapter will help us see this more. Before we get there, however, what is the main lesson of this chapter? Since children are already pure love they will respond best when we give them love, caring, good attention, understanding. Since they are already naturally full of joy and wonder (which is also the natural capacity to reach out and learn) we want to interfere with that feeling as little as possible. Since those feelings are close to being pure and uncontaminated we want to do our best not to contaminate them with our own thinking [See Chapter III].

A Miami family therapist perhaps puts it best: "Where parents go wrong is they look at their children and see something incomplete, and they feel like they have to fix it. But it's impossible to complete something that is already perfectly complete. When parents begin to see that they're pretty nice people and have something nice to give and relax a little and get a nice feeling back, they then look at the child and see a different person. They see a child that has the capacity to grow, to learn, to give love, to behave well. Kids, like all human beings, are geared to behaving well, to learning naturally. . . If the parent is able to calm down, that parent can see the child's potential and provide a safe, nonjudgmental, respectful, loving feeling in the home to bring it out in them. Parents are guides. *Rather than see the incomplete, see that there is nothing wrong with our children except our own perceptions. See them with a sense of wonder. See them as a limitless, infinite capacity to grow.*"

Remember: We do not have to do anything to make our children become good kids. They already are!

III. WE ARE WHAT WE THINK

Judy and I agreed to take in a temporary foster child, twelve years old. Jennifer [her name has been changed here] and her mother had had a terrible fight. Allegedly Jen had been beaten badly. We heard that her mother's boyfriend had been abusing Jen. Encouraged by her thirteen-year-old boyfriend, Jen called the state department of social services and was temporarily removed from her home. She'd been virtually living on the streets.

It did not take us long to learn that Jen had developed some pretty bad habits. We caught her in a lie. Then another. Then another. She stole some money to support her cigarette addiction. She manipulated everyone around her to get what she wanted. When Judy caught her in the lies and pointed them out to her she became angry. "You know too many people around here!" she snapped.

Her entire life seemed to consist of lying, cheating, stealing, manipulating.

Jen wanted to be with her real father. Her father wanted her too yet was afraid to take her in because he was also trying to gain custody of his three younger children and was not in good health. He also knew that given Jen's propensity for being on the streets he didn't have the parenting skills to keep Jen under control. In our presence he kindly lectured Jen about his fears and how she would have to give him assurance that he could take her in without problems. Jen promised to be responsible.

It took only a day for us to catch her in another lie—something about needing to go to a friend's house to do a special school project "on Hebrews." When we checked we discovered the school knew nothing of this project. (She knew we were Jewish. Pretty clever.) Next, Jen invited her mother over to our house despite that the state forbade her to see her mother except in their offices under their supervision. Jen then ran out on our daughter, Jaime, who was looking after her when we were out having a teacher conference about Jaime's progress.

The next day Jen was scheduled to go to court to learn where she would be placed. For some reason I woke up in the middle of the night feeling incredible clarity about Jen's problem:

Nothing, absolutely nothing was wrong with Jen, except for her thinking.

Jennifer's thinking was off kilter. In other words, but for her thinking she would be a perfectly normal functioning twelve year old—a fine kid. Destructive conditions at home may have helped precipitate her messed up thinking, but the only part of Jen that was "damaged" was the way she used her thinking process, and that could always change. I saw it so clearly!

Yet, nothing in the entire social services system was designed to help Jen or any other young people understand how their thinking was getting them into trouble, so it could change.

THOUGHT IS THE KEY

If not for their thinking all teenagers would be wonderful human beings. Something lies behind their presenting behavior. Behind all behavior problems lies a certain type of thinking.

Remember from the last chapter that hidden beneath the off-kilter thinking that makes people feel bad and gets them into trouble lies that glowing ember of the pure love and health that they brought with them into the world? They then learned to think their way away from it.

The only thing keeping kids from seeing and being in touch with their beautiful, inner, healthy, loving energy *deep inside them is their own thinking—no matter how bad or problematic their behavior.*[*]

CHILDREN ARE ALWAYS DOING THEIR BEST

What we see of our children's behavior is the way they have learned to respond to life. This learning is their own thinking. In other words, they created their own way of way of seeing the world from how they were treated and what they were told and what they took in as they were growing up, and they are just trying to respond the best way they know how. They don't know how to respond in any other way. *They are doing the best they know how at the time, given the way they see things. In that sense they are innocent.* Jen was innocent. She didn't know what else to do; she didn't know how else to respond.

When Judy and I were caught up in Jaime's antics [Chapter I] and didn't know how to respond well we, too, were innocent because we didn't see any other way at the time. Jaime was innocent because she didn't know any other way at that time. Now she does, therefore she acts completely differently. So do we.

So, besides going out of our way to show Jaime love, we also started to help Jaime take a look at how she was using her power of thought and how that thinking was affecting her. She saw it! This changed the entire tenor of our relationship.

---

[*]Note: I know some would argue that in some cases physical problems or chemical imbalances or A.D.H.D and other disorders cause some kids to behave badly, and I do not dispute this. It is also conceivable, however, that the thinking could have preceded the imbalance or disorder, or that people's thinking stands between the imbalance or disorder and the behavior, causing it to be manifested in different ways.

Alas, with Jen we did not have time to put this into practice. Sadly, she was placed in a permanent foster home.

Suppose all parents understood not only how to draw out the innate health in their children, but also how to help their children look at how they are using their thinking, so their feelings and behaviors would follow like dominoes, and change in constructive ways. Unfortunately, instead, many of us find ourselves troubled by our children's behavior, unable to find the feeling in our hearts we need to help our children see their thinking.

What can we do when we're in this position? We first need to understand what makes kids behave as they do. *Our understanding of why children behave the way they do (and why we behave as we do) will determine our effectiveness and satisfaction in dealing with them.*

WHY KIDS BEHAVE AS THEY DO

If we accept the premise from the last chapter that children are not born insecure or with spiteful or troubled behavior, how do they come up with it? If children have wisdom and common sense inside them, why don't they often use it?

Here's why: From the moment we're born we start forgetting that we have it. Things happen to us. We form thoughts about those events, situations and circumstances. Our parents tell us things and we form thoughts about what they tell us. This process is a necessary part of life. We develop a way of thinking that helps us make sense out of the world.

Such thinking causes us to see ourselves in certain ways. Some thoughts can make us feel insecure. Some can make us afraid. Some thoughts can make us judgmental of others. Some can make us feel bad. Some can make us angry. Some thoughts can make us feel we have to behave

22

in certain ways to maintain what we've learned to think about ourselves. Many of these thoughts take us away from our natural state of well-being and self-esteem. Many thoughts get so loud in our heads we can no longer hear our inner wisdom and common sense.

In short, innocently, we have begun to think ourselves away from our health.

No one does this intentionally. It just seems to happen to all of us as we live and grow.

One of the secrets to whether we will raise children in healthy, productive, satisfying, joyful ways—and one of the secrets to our own happiness and peace of mind—is to understand that *if we could somehow get those unproductive thoughts out of the way or at least not take them seriously, the inner, natural state would automatically rise to the surface.*

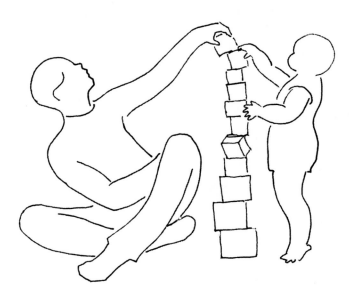

Dr. Roger Mills likened it to holding a cork under water. The cork is buoyant, so it is always trying to rise to the surface. Our hand is the only thing keeping the cork down; our thinking is the only thing keeping our innate health and wisdom down. This implies we don't have to *do* anything except get out of our own way. All we have to do is let go of the cork and it will naturally rise on its own. All we have to do is ignore, let go of, dismiss, forget about or not take seriously the thoughts keeping those natural, inner feelings submerged and it will appear for us, because it never really went anywhere in the first place.

If this notion seems vague or impractical or too simple or too complex or off the subject of raising kids at this point, fear not. Concern is only another of those thoughts that can get in the way. As this book unfolds so will your understanding of how this works and how it is possible to apply this in day-to-day situations. What we are talking about here is the foundation for everything that follows.

Children act out or troubled only because the thinking they have taken on has made them lose touch with their natural state of well-being and common sense. Their thinking has made it appear to them that they should act exactly as they are. In other words, given what they believe and how the world looks to them at that moment they have no other choice but to feel and act in that way. This is why they are always doing the best they know at the time.

What, then, does this suggest we do?

When we step back and look at it, what comes to mind is plain common sense. If our children have natural health and wisdom already inside them, and if they also have certain thoughts that create insecurities that lead them to act in troubling ways, two things need to happen:

1. We could help this inner, natural state to emerge and their own wisdom and common sense to guide them;

2. We could help them understand how not to let their negative or insecure thoughts get in their way.

To accomplish these would take us 90% along the road to successful parenting. (I made that percentage up. I mean a whole lot!)

CREATING INSECURE THINKING

When our children are young, if we yell at them and put them down or nag them and criticize them and tell them they're not okay we are inadvertently teaching them to have insecure thoughts about themselves. They then take them on and *become those thoughts*.

When schools tell kids they won't fit in or they won't do well or they will have trouble learning or that they're troublemakers, if young people believe it they will think it themselves; they will think that is who they are. This keeps them looking outside themselves for the answer about who they are.

This leads to an insecure set of beliefs. If parents are always telling a kid that he's stupid, and then something happens to fit into those beliefs, such as getting an "F" on a test, he may think something like, "They must be right, I am stupid." Those beliefs get reinforced. Once those beliefs are entrenched and become a pattern, then even when something comes along that contradicts it, such as getting an "A" the kid may think something like, "Oh, that was just a fluke," and write it off. So once those beliefs are locked in, no matter what comes along it confirms and validates them. No matter what comes along those kids will still think they are stupid and act as if they really are. The world then reacts to them accordingly which, in turn, reinforces it. A vicious downward thinking cycle develops.

This is what moves children and other people away from recognizing their natural state.

Don't forget, we parents have also picked up such beliefs. Where did we get them? From our parents! Then without being aware of it we pass them along to our children. For example, if your mother was a worrier you likely picked up this worry and passed it along like a baton in a relay race. Probably you're not passing it along in the exact way, but in some way you may be. It then gets programmed into our children's brains as it was inadvertently programmed into ours.

Dr. George Pransky says our children pick up "'as if worlds" from us. This means we begin to go through life *as if* certain things about life are most important. If our parents inadvertently taught us by their actions that we should go through life *as if* money is important, we begin to see a lot of things in life in terms of money.

When my son was a freshman in college and about to go to his first prom, he said to his mother that he couldn't believe how expensive it was to rent the tux and pay for admission. Judy said, "Dave, since when did you get so concerned about money? Where did you get that from?"

Without batting an eyelash, he said, "From dad!"

Ugh! A humbling moment.

And I know where I got it from: my mother! (Bless her heart, she was very sweet and loving in most all other ways.) My father, on the other hand, was always exceptionally generous and money never seemed to be an issue to him. But he never talked about money and my mother did—a lot. She grew up in a family that, during the depression, struggled hard to make ends meet. Interestingly, my father also grew up in a family that struggled during the depression but his parents could barely speak English and he was mostly off making it on his own, so he picked up different thoughts about money. Anyway, my mother innocently took it on as her solemn duty to make sure we saved every day through bargain shopping, etc., so we would have enough money for important things. (Is it a coincidence that my mother prided herself on being frugal?) And I unknowingly and innocently picked it up and started to see much of my life as if money was enormously important. Then I graciously passed it along to my son.

My mother would have said, "Of course it's important to save every penny. That's why we've gotten by like we have!" No one would be able to talk her out of it because that was "reality" to her. Yet, other people do not think of money that way. They might be relaxed about money, or they might see abundance and not worry about it. But some of those people might go through life as if power or prestige were the all-important thing in life—or a million other things that a million other people think are important

Innocently we pick up such things from our parents. We may even take them on in a way our parents never intended, but they become our own. That's the point: They become our own. We own them now.

Of course I picked up other things from my parents, too. To my father, "family" was *the* most important thing in the world, even more important than sports. Family was very strong for my mother too, so I also came to see the world in terms of the importance of family, which is great—until I try to shove family obligations down my kids' throats, no matter what is going on with them at the time.

Judy does not understand "time." In her family of origin her parents went about their business until they finished whatever they were doing, so they were rarely on time for things. I didn't even start counting that Judy was late until after an hour has passed. That she was continually late drove our kids crazy. Of course our kids said they would never do that to their kids, and they took pride in not being that way themselves. But both of them

27

procrastinated until the very last moment to do what they needed to do, so they were continually in a mad, hurried, harried, frustrated dash to get somewhere on time. This reflects how insidious this all is.

Another parent will imply that we should go through life *as if* not backing down from anyone is important. That kid will likely end up in a lot of fights.

Another parent will say that *life is all about* trusting people. This sounds good—until that kid ends up trusting everyone to the point of being taken advantage of.

For other parents *life is all about* hard work. This sounds good too—until some become workaholics. For others *life is all about* survival—doing anything you need to do to survive. We could go on and on.

We parents might ask ourselves what we picked up from our parents that we might be inadvertently passing along to our children. Yet, for every one we know about there is at least another that we have no idea about that we're also carrying with us and passing along. We could call this a "blind spot." We all have them. Our partners or friends or close work associates could probably tell us what they are. We could tell them theirs, but we often can't see our own. They are hidden from us (which is why they are blind spots), but we still think them unknowingly.

The importance of this for raising our children cannot be overstated. This is how our children's programmed, habitual thinking develops. *Out of this habitual, programmed thinking they then see the world, and out of how they see the world they think, feel and act.*

COLORING OUR WORLDS

George Pransky tells a story of how he and his wife once went camping in the woods with another couple. His usually laid-back friend demanded they hurry up and get wood for the fire. George couldn't figure out why his friend was acting as if there was such a rush, but he went along with him. George wanted to stop and see some of the beautiful scenery in the great Northwest but his friend told him there wasn't time; they had to quickly find firewood and get it back to the campsite. When they arrived back at the campsite their partners were lying down relaxing and reading, and his friend blasted in and tried to hurry everyone up to get the campfire going.

His wife said, "I'm really not ready to move just yet."

Then she looked up at him and asked, "Why are you wearing your sunglasses?"

He put his hand to his eyes, bumped into them, looked puzzled, then took them off and said, "Whoa, it's early!"

He thought it was getting dark, and because it was late they'd better quickly snap to it and get the fire going. The sunglasses he didn't know he was wearing colored the way he saw everything, which in turn colored the way he felt, which in turn colored the way he acted.

This is what happens to us all the time. This is what happens with our kids. We are all looking out of different colored lenses and acting *as if* what we are seeing is the way life really is.

Any of us who have ever put on a pair of strangely-colored sunglasses, such as yellow, at first sees the world looking very strange. But if we keep them on for a long time we begin to get used to it and that vision of the world begins to look "normal." This is what happens with our habitual thinking.

Everyone sees the world through a different pair of colored lenses they are not aware they have on. Yet they think what they're seeing is *the way it really is!* And for everyone it is different. This explains why there are so many fights, arguments and disagreements. *Everyone is living in a separate world, a separate reality, that they each think is right.*

So are our kids. Our kids live in separate worlds from us. They therefore think differently, feel differently and act differently than we do. Just as we think our world is right, so they think theirs is right. No wonder we have so many conflicts!

We and our children may have some similarities in our ways of thinking, but we all have different experiences and interpret those experiences very differently.

WHAT TO DO?

What does this suggest about dealing with our kids?

First, we want to be a little careful about how seriously we take our own thinking. If we pay very close attention we might be able to tell when a habitual pattern has become programmed in us and rears its head. It sounds all too familiar. If we see it we may want to be a little more

30

careful about what we lay on our kids, because it comes from our own "reality" of what we think is important.

Second, we want to understand that when we react to children in a negative way that becomes a pattern, our children can pick up a similar thinking pattern for themselves. They then act out of that pattern. So if we want kids who behave well we might want to watch how we think and behave. For example, if we tend to react with anger to whatever they do wrong, our kids may pick up a tendency to react with anger when they encounter something they don't like.

One might ask, if we go out of our way not to program negativity, what will be left? What will remain? What remains is their natural health and wisdom. If we do not inject negativity the natural well-being and self-esteem rises to the surface because it never went anywhere in the first place. The veil is merely lifted off it. Negative thoughts are the only thing keeping the naturally positive feelings hidden. In other words, we don't have to go out of our way to think positively because if we're not thinking negatively the positive will automatically be there.

It helps to be mindful that our children act based on their thinking and much of their thinking stems from what they have been innocently exposed to and learned. We and our children are both innocently caught up in the web through which we each now see. Since no one is perfect—certainly including this author/parent—it is helpful to realize that the less we treat our kids in ways that breed negative, unhealthy, destructive or problematic thinking the less our children will have a tendency to act out of what becomes programmed, habitual thinking for them.

As an alternative we can watch our children in their thought patterns. We can watch ourselves in our thought patterns. We don't have to take either too seriously because those patterns are only "real" to each of us because of the different ways we both happen to see it.

"But if we're bothered, how can we let go of our thoughts of bother?"

So long as we're seeing "reality," we're not going to be able to let go of those thoughts. It takes seeing a bigger picture. For example, suppose you were bothered by what your daughter was doing and got angry at her and started yelling at her. That's real, right? Now suppose in the middle of yelling at her, she fainted. Would not your thinking about her and what she was up to change markedly in that moment? Or what if you found out your son only had another year to live? Suddenly leaving clothes scattered around the house doesn't bother us so much anymore. We only have thoughts of bother or upset when we're not thinking about something else. That's how "real" it is.

It is really all an illusion made up by the way we use our own thinking. To truly realize this can be quite humbling. [More on this in the next chapter]

IV. STATES OF MIND -- MOODS

I come home from a hard day's work. I'm tired. I'm crabby. I'm snappy. I see that Jaime has once again dropped her books and jacket and boots and everything else she owns right in front of the door. I grumble to myself, "This girl has learned nothing! She's doing it to me again! I've been totally incapable of teaching her responsibility." I spot her upstairs and yell, "Jaime, how many times do I have to tell you to get this crap out of here!" She yaps back and makes another excuse.

It's the weekend. I wake up calm and relaxed, in good spirits. I walk downstairs and notice Jaime has again left her stuff in the hallway. I smile. It's so her! When I see her I say cheerfully, "Hey Jaims, how about moving your stuff?" She says, "Okay dad, sorry," and picks it up.

Same books, same coat, same hallway; different moods, different view, different outcomes.

In a low mood what she did speaks to the very heart of my capability as a parent and to her incapability as a kid. In a good mood it's water off a duck's back.

MOODS AFFECT ACTION

Being effective and successful as a parent has more to do with a parent's state of mind than whether the parent knows parenting techniques.

When parents are upset or in low moods they tend to forget any parenting technique they know. At such times, even if they had the presence of mind to use the technique it would not necessarily come out right because a bad feeling seeps through and negates its usefulness—because kids react more to the feeling.

In a good mood, when spirits are high, at those times the parent's mood elevates the feeling and communication and overrides naturally the need for techniques.

More than techniques parents need an understanding of states of mind and their effect on our parenting at any given time. *Children respond better when we deal with them from a responsive, secure frame of mind.*

At any given moment every human being is in one of two states of mind: a secure, responsive state, or an insecure, reactive state. Of course there are many varying degrees but there also seems to be a line that, once crossed, puts us in one state or the other. We all know what both states feel like. We have all visited both. We go up and down and back and forth between these states continuously during the day. We can tell the difference.

In the insecure, reactive state we tend to act out of fear and insecurity. We seem to have a lot of knee-jerk reactions. We feel threatened.

In the secure, responsive state we tend to act out of security and wisdom that tells us what is best. We keep our bearings.

Moods are part of the human condition. Each mood is a different level of consciousness through which we see our children and what they are up to. We react according to what we see at each of these levels. We react to our children according the mood we're in at the time, because it is what we see at that time.

Our moods go up and down all the time like the ocean has tides. When up, we're relaxed, we're lighthearted, we listen more. When down, we see those around us in a negative way; we overreact.

DIFFERENT MOODS, DIFFERENT PEOPLE

A little-realized fact is that we are completely different people in low, reactive moods than in high, responsive moods. We are Dr. Jekyll and Mr. Hyde. If someone met you for the first time when you were in a low mood, and someone else met you for the first time when you were in a high mood, and the two people then got together and described to each other your personality and what you were like, they would each think they were describing two completely different people.

When we act out of one state as opposed to the other what we say and do is completely different and the results are completely different.

The state of mind we are in when interacting with our children at any given time will determine how effectively we will deal with them. Since we naturally go in and out of each of these states—up and down in our many moods all day long—and since we can only do so much about being in those moods, the key becomes from which state of mind would we rather talk, act, or make decisions?

MOOD AWARENESS

First, it is helpful to simply be aware of which state of mind we are in at any given time. We can tell which state we're in by how we feel. If we're feeling great, we're in the secure, responsive state; if we're feeling lousy or low or angry or frantic or fearful we've slid into the insecure, reactive state. Noticing how we feel when we're about to confront or talk to our kids provides our first signal about how to proceed.

In a negative, reactive state, even the smallest problem seems large. It is difficult to see solutions. In the secure, responsive state, problems don't look so overwhelming. We see the way out. Things look hopeful. Problems seem more manageable. In fact, some problems that loomed large in a negative, reactive state don't even look like problems from a more positive state. Which is "reality?"

Both, or neither.

Our kids also jump back and forth between these two states—sometimes many times a day.

The best time to deal with our kids, then, especially in trying to help them learn something, is when we're both in positive, open, responsive states. In negative, reactive moods we simply do not come across well. Our kids will react by getting a little frightened or insecure and will resist what we say. In a low state they are automatically closed off to whatever anyone tries to tell them. Their walls go up to protect themselves.

MOOD THINKING AND ACTION

So what do we do when we're in a low state and must get something across to our kids?

The best thing to do in an insecure, reactive state or low mood is nothing, or as little as we can possibly get away with.

All we have to do is wait it out. If we are in a low mood, our mood is guaranteed to rise eventually. (If in a high mood, our mood will drop eventually.) Very few situations are so urgent that they must be dealt with at that moment, although the lower our mood the more urgent it looks. In most cases we have about eighteen years to be with our kids to help them learn from us. How much time will we lose if we wait out a low mood before acting? We nearly always have a second chance. Will we take it?

Needless to say, if a child is in danger or an emergency is at hand it doesn't matter what kind of mood we're in. Of course the danger at the moment must always be dealt with instantly. But when neither danger nor an emergency is present, if we are in a low state and need to teach something about their behavior, it really helps to stop, bite our tongues, step back for a while and regain perspective—for as long as it takes—until we feel a healthier state of mind and wisdom kick in. Then we can deal with it.

Likewise, if our kids are in low moods they first need to calm down enough to hear what we have to say, so they may need to be separated from us or the situation for a while until they regain their bearings. When spirits have risen on both sides we then get together and talk from a more productive perspective.

Put simply, we are wasting our time and energy trying to deal with our children when either of us is in a low state. Plus, the more we do it the more it harms the relationship.

If we do not have good feelings in the moment or if we're overwrought or wound up about something or thinking thoughts about how bad or how difficult our kids are, those are the worst times to deal with our children. Our thinking and our moods are essentially one and the same; our thinking is tied up with our moods. *Low moods equal low-quality thoughts.* When feeling low or frantic or angry, etc. it is especially helpful to take the space to clear our heads in whatever way it works for us.

When caught up in our emotions we're the ones who need the "time out!"

Some of us may have to completely remove ourselves for a while until we feel more calm and able to have thoughts from that calmer place within us, so we may need to walk around the block (at least figuratively). Some of us may have to remove our child for a while until s/he calms down. Some of us may have to wait out an extended bad mood. Some may have to count to ten. Whatever it takes is different for each individual. If we want to deal constructively, however, it is always best to deal with the child when both of us are in a calm, rational frame of mind.

Sometimes we may have say to a child (something like), "I'm too upset to deal with this right now. We'll talk later." Sometimes we may have to say (something like), "It looks like you need to calm down some before we talk about this, so we'll talk about it later."

MAKING ADJUSTMENTS

The problem is that in low moods we feel *compelled* to say something or take action. However, if we recognize how destructive this could be, that recognition alone may be enough to hold our tongues or fists. The adjustment is to back off and wait.

In summary, what do we do when we cannot seem to find that responsive state of mind, or find that loving, caring, warm feeling for our child in the moment?

1. The first thing is recognize when we are in an insecure, reactive state or a low mood. This is not so difficult once we begin to pay attention to how we are feeling. Remember, our feelings always tell us which state we are in at any given time. Remember too, that what we are feeling is the climate we're creating at the moment.

2 (a). If our feeling tells us we're in a secure, responsive state, it serves as a signal to us—a green light, so to speak—that it is okay to go ahead and act, because at that time we can pretty much trust whatever naturally

comes up to deal with a situation. [More on this in Chapter VI.]

2 (b). If our feeling tells us we're in a low, reactive state, it serves as a signal—a red light—to stop and wait. In this state it is best not to try to teach anything to our children or discipline them at that moment. It is best to clear our heads, get ourselves back on track and allow wisdom to speak.

2 (c). If we are unsure of our feeling, it serves as a yellow light: slow down and proceed with caution.

It never helps to breed more insecurity. If we are upset and our child does something that upsets us even more, any action we take at that time will make the child feel more insecure. Conversely, backing off and clearing our heads gets us back on track.

Sometimes this is easier said than done. If a single parent, for example, has a screaming little kid on her hands, has no relatives in the vicinity to help bail her out, doesn't have the money to hire a babysitter for an hour or two, has a one room apartment and there's a blizzard outside so she can't take her kid out for a walk, it can be awfully difficult. However, even during those times, we could pay attention to our feeling and know it means we won't react well at that moment, but this mood will eventually pass. If we can hold ourselves together long enough to make sure the kid is all right, has her biological needs tended to and is safe, if the kid still insists on screaming we can reassure her that we need to be by ourselves for a little while but we'll be back, and then we might put on headphones or stick cotton in our ears and read a good book or take a hot bath or do whatever it takes to calm ourselves so we can go back to her in a good frame of mind.

Does this mean ignoring or neglecting the child? Absolutely not! Even at those times we must still keep alert enough to the child to prevent any disasters. All this means is, within the parameters of safety, we do as little as we can possibly get away with and for ourselves whatever will help to improve our own state of mind.

MOOD SPIRALS

If we find ourselves saying, "I can't do this!", or "I'm a failure as a parent," this is just our low mood talking. We cannot trust our thinking in low moods. At that moment we probably can't do very well, but we also need to realize that such a statement reflects only a passing thought at that moment—if we let it pass. If we get scared we said it and start dwelling on it and believe it has implications beyond our mood at the moment—that it speaks to the very heart of our inability as a parent and means we never should have had children in the first place—then we will start to believe it. We make it true and start to live it. But it's *only a thought* that popped into our heads! So we can either let it pass through and not take it seriously, or we can dwell on it and make it real. We decide.

MOODS IN ACTION

In my book, *Modello*, about how this inside-out approach changed lives in two low-income, inner-city housing projects, I described a situation where moods came into play concerning a parent I called Carrie Mae. Carrie Mae was a nice woman who loved her children. She also had a violent temper. When her temper got riled up she was known to "go off" on anyone, anywhere, especially on her own kids, and particularly when something bad would happen in school. At those times she was known to grab her belt, storm over to the school and "wail away" on her kid even in front of the principal.

One day the principal phoned. Her son (in sixth grade) had just pulled a knife on another kid in school. Carrie

Mae became livid. She grabbed her belt and stormed over to school.

But she had been learning about moods! Halfway to the school, something popped into her head: "Wait a minute. I'm in a really bad mood right now. I'd better watch it."

When she arrived at the school she simply picked up her son, brought him home, put him in his room, went to a friend's house and stayed there for three hours. She stayed until she once again felt that loving, caring feeling for her son.

She then went back to him and in a calm, caring tone said something like, "Honey, can you tell me what was going on with you, pulling a knife and all? Has something been going on over at school?"

Shocked that he wasn't being beaten, her son whimpered, "Yeah, these boys have been picking on me and I was really scared and I didn't know what to do."

Carrie Mae had no idea this was happening. She had never taken the time to listen.

They both broke down and cried. They had a tremendous breakthrough in their relationship. And it lasted.

This is the power of understanding moods.

TAKING RESPONSIBILITY FOR WHAT HAPPENS IN OUR MOODS

Given the vast improvements in our own relationship with Jaime we began to realize the only time we fell out of our wonderful feelings for each other was when we were in low moods. We all had our moments of low moods, of course, but now we knew enough to ride them out and not take personally what anyone said when in them. We knew what we saw in our low mood thinking was not "real"— unless we made it be. What is real is the inner health and well-being and wisdom and common sense that gets brought out through love and understanding.

We sure wouldn't want our loved ones to take too seriously some of the things we've said and done in our low moods, so would it also not be wise to take too personally what they throw at us at those times? Remember, such thinking will look completely different later when our mood rises, so we would do well not to act on what we're seeing at those times.

As George Pransky says, our relationship with our children is like a savings account. When we feel closer we put in deposits. When we feel more distant we make withdrawals. In a secure, responsive state we naturally make deposits. In insecure, reactive states we make withdrawals—unless we are aware we're about to make a withdrawal if we act on what we're thinking or open our big mouths.

To take responsibility for our own mood-thinking and how it affects our subsequent actions is one of the most productive, practical things we can do as parents.

KIDS UNDERSTAND MOODS

With Katie's husband away on business for a couple of weeks she was left to take care of her two kids. Both kids were involved in dance lessons, gymnastics and other sports, and Kate had to do all the transporting, organizing and running around by herself. She was beat and grumpy.

At the dinner table that night her kids were in great moods. Katie was not! All evening long she barked out orders for them to do this and that, with no kindness or caring in her voice.

"Take your vitamins!" she barked.

"Mom."

"What?"

"Go to bed. "

Her mother paused for a moment, stunned, then as if on automatic pilot, she nodded, "Okay" and made a beeline to the bedroom.

Intuitively, she knew her kids knew a lot more than she did at that moment.

* * *

A friend's child was having so much fun at daycare that when her mother came to pick her up she did not want to leave. The mother, who was rushed and in a low mood, wanted her child to come along–now!

The child said, "I'm not going."

"Yes you are."

"Nope,' she said, shaking her head.

"Yes you are! Come along right now!"

"You're not my mommy!" her daughter said with a scowl.

"What? Well, maybe you're not my daughter."

"You can't say that!"

"Why not?"

"Because I'm going to like you later."

V. WHAT PROBLEM BEHAVIOR IS

Our son, who was then seventeen, and Judy and I took a trip to visit colleges. David was in a foul mood and taking it out on us. We knew it was only a profoundly low mood, but it was wearing on our nerves.

I was driving and to him I could do nothing right. He would criticize me and yap at me for practically every move I made.

"Would you like to drive, Dave?"

"No."

"Well, if you're not willing to drive, don't criticize my driving then."

I tried to keep my spirits high and make light of it, but finally he said something enormously rude and nasty, and it really got to me. In other words, I lost myself.

I told him I didn't appreciate what he said, and I didn't think I deserved it. Unfortunately, I let it put me into a low mood. It gripped me and I couldn't seem to let it go. So I separated myself from him to clear my head. We stopped to eat and I decided that either he was going to have to change or I wanted out. They could put me on a bus and I'd go back home. I thought about it over lunch and told Judy that's what I wanted to do.

During lunch David decided to stay in the car to take a nap instead of eating. We got back in the car with Judy driving. I hadn't had a chance to say anything to Dave yet because he was just waking up. Then because we couldn't seem to find our way back onto the highway David started making rude comments to Judy.

She said, "That's it! I'm out of here!" and started driving toward the freeway to head home. "If you want to get out and stay, get out!"

Dave said, "Okay, let me out. I'll stay here myself."

Judy called his bluff. She pulled over and said, "Okay, get out!"

Dave didn't move.

By this time I had calmed down myself and said, "David, don't you see what you're doing to people? I had just asked mom to put me on a bus and that I'd go because I didn't want to take this stuff from you anymore and, apparently, mom isn't going to take it any more either."

He said something to the effect that we were both stupid drivers.

I said, "But you said you weren't willing to drive! We don't know where we're going. We've never been here before. We're trying to find our way around. It's not so easy in a strange place. The idea is not to sit back and judge and criticize, but to enter into a partnership with us so together we can figure out where we're going and how to do it best. That's how people help each other out."

I saw him soften a bit.

I continued. "Look, mom's about to leave here, and that will be all for this trip, so if that's what you really want, we can do that, but maybe, instead, would you be willing to commit yourself to treat us with respect for at least the rest of this trip?"

He uttered a faint, "Yes."

I turned to Judy. "Do you accept that?"

She said, "Yes."

The rest of our trip went great! Dave slipped a few times but we reminded him about his commitment and that seemed to calm him down.

Later, he confided in us how scared he was about visiting colleges and the prospect of being far away from home. He was taking it out on the place he felt safest—us! This was his tendency. Whenever he felt insecure about anything he took it out on us.

BAD APPLES?

What is bad behavior?

Bad behavior is nothing more than people acting out of insecurity.

When people lack understanding they tend to be more insecure. When people are in low moods they tend to be more insecure. When people have organic problems that irritate behavior centers in the brain they tend to get frightened and act out (these people may also lack more controls). David happened to have all three going on inside him and he was frightened. Since showing fear is not cool (after all, he was a teenager and a very cool one at that), he acted out.

It is extremely important for parents to realize that everything we call "bad behavior," "troublesome behavior," "troubled behavior" boils down to people acting out of insecurity.

This has enormous implications. By acting in troublesome or troubling ways children are not trying to nail us or do something bad to us. They are only acting out of insecurity. They're frightened for some reason and at that time they don't know any other way to be. The way they act at those times is the only thing that makes sense to them, and they may not have a clue why they're doing it. In other words, it's the best they know how to do at that time.

INSECURITY AND INNOCENCE

If every child is always doing the best s/he knows how at the time given the way s/he sees things, *children are acting out of innocence.*

So are we! We parents are only doing the best we know how at the time. We are innocent too. We can relax a little and not take ourselves too seriously.

47

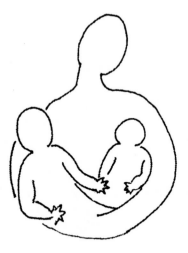

Children are not born with insecurity. It is something they have to learn. Usually they learn it from us, then sometimes from their close relatives, then from peers and school. No one tries to teach insecurity; that is the last thing we want. Yet, in our innocence we sometimes do and say things that contribute to it.

As stated earlier, children are born into a world filled with wonder. Everything is new. There are so many new things to see, so many new smells, so many sounds, tastes and a whole world to touch! It is the greatest amusement park imaginable. If babies start to feel physically uncomfortable they begin to cry. This is perfectly natural. Whatever it is—a hurting tummy, a yucky diaper—doesn't feel good and crying is a natural response. The baby also soon learns that a cry will usually send a parent to the rescue, and that feels nice.

Tiny newborns begin to cry and we comfort them and give them understanding, and we keep doing that until one day our child is crying for a really long time and we get irritated (because we're in a low mood or we're frightened because we don't know what to do), and we may yap at the baby in a louder voice with an edge, and it scares her. Then she cries louder and the cycle begins. The baby thinks to herself, "Whoa, what's this!? I think I'd better watch out here. All is not as it seems." Or maybe the parent stops coming around when she's crying. What used to work doesn't anymore.

Unless babies learn insecurity quite early in abusive or neglectful homes, in most homes they probably don't learn much insecurity until they begin to move around. Then they learn to crawl. Now they can get places, and suddenly their world vastly expands. They can get into things. "Yes!" they shout with glee.

When the crawler or toddler grabs certain items the parents stop him and scold him, or sometimes slap him. The world has changed and he doesn't understand it so well anymore. It's confusing. It can be scary. Insecurity begins to creep in.

When the child begins to walk at first everyone is so thrilled—but the world vastly expands again, opening up a new world of possible things to get into, and the cycle escalates.

Then the child begins to talk and everyone is so excited. Then one day she apparently opens her mouth at the wrong time or the wrong thing comes out and suddenly it seems that, at times, talking is no good and everything becomes so confusing. Insecurity abounds.

Much insecurity, then, seems to occur out of complete innocence, simply by what we learn as we grow. There is almost no way parents can avoid having their children develop some insecurities. The more we can help them feel secure, however, despite the difficulties they get into, the better off they are. The better off we are.

When children feel insecure or fearful they act in strange ways—just as we do. Children act in any way they think will make the fear and insecurity go away, only they are not aware they are thinking it. The flaw in this thinking is the insecurity usually does not go away. In fact, the way kids act when they are insecure usually makes things worse, just as when we act out of insecurity or fear we make things worse.

If our children knew better they would do better. No one wants pain. Nobody likes the pain their actions cause, but they don't know how to do it any differently at the time.

INSECURITY AS THOUGHT

Behind all insecurity is thought. At the root lies thought. *Thought can change.*

When kids are acting out, the key for parents is to realize how they are seeing their children at those times. We could see the kid as purposely giving us a hard time, or we could see him as insecure and just acting out his insecurity without knowing any other way to do it at the time.

Suppose we see the kid as giving us a hard time. How would we react?

Suppose we see the kid as insecure and trying in any way he can to compensate for it. Would we react differently?

From each of those different vantage points we would automatically treat the kid differently. What would be our natural inclination if we thought our kid was out to get us or purposely trying to do wrong, compared with if we thought our child was hurting inside and afraid?

If an infant has a crying fit, and his little arms flail away and he hits us in the eye and it really hurts, we don't hold it against the baby.

If a toddler, in a crying fit, little legs kicking away, kicks us in the shins and it really hurts, would we hold it against her?

If a teenager, in a fit of rage, hormones kicking away, puts his fist through the wall, do we hold it against him? More often than not, we do.

Yet it's all insecurity.

If we see bad behavior as willful we tend to want to control and punish. If we see bad behavior as acting out of insecurity we might ask ourselves how we can help take away his or her insecure thoughts.

MANIFESTATIONS OF INSECURITY

Some kids have angry and violent responses. Some kids get sad and depressed. Some kids cheat and steal. Some kids yell and scream. Some kids get sneaky. Some kids take drugs and drink to excess. Some kids pick on others and do them harm. Some kids become sex abusers. Some kids grow up to physically or emotionally abuse their own kids or their spouses. Some kids get judgmental and put down their parents for the way they drive.

The reason? They are all acting out of insecurity in their own ways. It is not that they are trying to be that way; they do not understand anything else. Please, I am *not* saying this excuses their behavior [we will deal with that in future chapters]; I am only talking here about the way we see it.

WHAT TO DO?

How can we help them understand at a deeper level what is going on to help them feel more secure?

The first thing is not to take personally what they are doing. If they are acting out of insecurity why would we take it personally? It's got nothing to do with us. It's them! If we don't take it personally we don't need to react at that level.

For my doctoral dissertation I studied the effects on participants after attending what was then called "Health Realization" training (now "The Three Principles"), which is what this book is based upon. I will never forget what a mother named Caroline told me regarding her son who had diabetes. He had been experiencing a lot of low blood sugar episodes, and one of the key symptoms of low blood sugar is irritability and not being in one's "right mind," so to speak. One of these fits occurred at 3:00 in the morning. Caroline went in to deal with him and it didn't go well. He said to her, "You're the worst thing that's ever happened to me!" Whoa! Caroline left his bedroom thinking, "Okay, that's about the worst thing I could hear." But what was she to do? Was she going to sit there and dwell on it and start tearing up? No, she realized that would be the stupidest thing she could do. It was only his low blood sugar talking. He wasn't in his right mind. There was no need to take it personally! She told me, "When you were a kid people would say, 'Don't take it personally,' and you would think, 'Well then, tell me how else to take it!'" But now that she had this understanding it became extremely clear why taking it personally doesn't help. The next day when her son's blood sugar rose he was as loving to her as ever.

The second thing is we can take a look at how we may be unknowingly passing on insecurity to our children. When the child exhibits inappropriate behavior the essence of the child is not at fault, only his thinking is. Thoughts lead to the feelings that lead to the behaviors that may lead us to have thoughts that make us react.

Dr. Roger Mills gave an example: If a parent harbors a strong belief that his children cannot be happy unless they are more athletic, artistic or educated the parent unknowingly passes those beliefs onto the child in an overly concerned, anxious way, which leads to insecurity. This child begins to think that his own well-being is contingent upon how well he does with respect to those "important" things. Then we get on him for not doing well. Yet, most people do not respond well to threats. Threats are external motivators and they're scary. People do not do well when they're "running scared."

For instance, if I can't let go of the thought that my child needs good grades, if she gets a poor grade I feel the tension and disappointment. Instead, I could observe my feelings. I could know that low or agitated feelings means my thinking is off track and can't be trusted at that moment. Of course it's natural to want our children to do well and succeed—we would love our child to get good grades—but other ways of seeing it exist at other levels of consciousness. One other way of seeing it is that she needs encouragement to do better. I could encourage her and let her know I really care. I could help her see how her wisdom could help her more. If she doesn't do well, at least I know I tried. Besides, she's good at other things. Everyone is good at something. Maybe it means she will develop her other talents. My daughter, Jaime, had dyslexia and it was very hard for her to read, and she didn't do so well in school (until her senior year), yet she was in the top echelon of her class at the Barbara Brennan School of Healing, which drew upon a completely different kind of intelligence.

SUMMARY

In summary, then, what does this suggest that we do as parents?

First, we want to look at ourselves to be sure we are raising our kids in a way that passes on to them as few of our insecurities as possible.

Then, if confronted with a problem behavior it is most helpful to see it as insecurity instead of as a personal attack or affront; that they're lost and can't see any better way at the time.

Seeing the behavior as insecurity will make us naturally respond in a more helpful way than seeing it as a willful, malicious act. Seeing it as insecurity makes us somehow want to help relieve that insecurity and help them see a better way.

Again, does this mean that we let them get away with everything? Absolutely not! It simply means if we see the child and the behavior differently we will naturally act differently.

The next chapter will help us see what to do.

VI. DISENGAGEMENT ~ TAPPING INTO WISDOM TO GUIDE INTERACTIONS

Some years ago a huge truck jammed itself under a bridge on Storrow Drive in Boston and became stuck. Traffic backed up for miles. No one knew what to do. They called in engineers.

Sitting in the car stuck in traffic an eight-year-old in one of the nearby cars turned to his father and said, "Dad, why don't they just let some of the air out of the tires?"

Out of the mouth of babes.

Our children have the capacity inside them to tap into wisdom if their minds are clear enough to hear it.

* * *

I am running barefoot on a beach scattered with many rocks. I keep my eyes fixed on the sand five feet ahead of me. I do not look where I put my feet. I step on no rocks.

What is going on? My feet seem to shift themselves as I move along. My natural intelligence seems to be guiding me.

If I get distracted I step on a rock and hurt my foot.

* * *

Our son, David was recruited to play basketball at a college in Massachusetts. Before he arrived the coach who recruited Dave left. A new coach came in. As a freshman David sat on the bench the entire season because the new coach played only seniors. Then, as a sophomore he was forced into a starting role. As I watched him play I'm thinking, "Gee, he's so much better than this. He's not taking any chances out there. Why isn't he playing up to his capability?"

I learned why. The coach was screaming at the players to try to get them to play right. It was working against him. David was playing to not make a mistake so he wouldn't be screamed at and benched, instead of playing from his heart and just letting the game flow.

I asked Dave if he thought he was playing to avoid mistakes now instead of getting into the flow of his own game. He said yes.

I asked him what he was thinking when he was scoring seemingly at will. He said, "Nothing."

I said, "Well, wouldn't it make sense to ignore the thinking? You know what you're capable of doing when you're not thinking, just getting into the flow. The other kind of thinking is just a distraction and takes you away from your game."

My telling him this meant nothing. He had to feel it for himself. By the middle of the season the team was continually losing and the coach increasingly was on their cases. Then one of the best players got kicked off the team for doing something stupid, the center became very ill when his mother died, so he was out of action, and the point guard decided to transfer.

I said, "Well Dave, figure it this way, the coach can't possibly expect you guys to win now, so you've got nothing to lose. You may as well just go out there and have a good time playing your game."

The next game David scored over twenty points, and the next, and the next. The only difference was his head cleared. The team even won a couple of games because everyone was playing so loosely. Then, thinking they had a chance to win again, the coach once again started screaming at them. Low and behold, the team started losing again. But for the rest of the season David never looked back. He had gained confidence in his own ability. He knew he could do it now, no matter what his coach did or said. Because his head had cleared he had clicked into a higher level of functioning, which made him play from the heart, tap into the purity of his skills and completely focus on the moment at hand, unencumbered by any extraneous thoughts such as how well he was doing.

Acting out of a clear head made Dave play at his peak. His wisdom took over. Ultimately, as he had in high school he scored over 1000 points in his college career in what amounted to only three years because he sat on the bench as a Freshman. He received an offer to play basketball professionally in Ireland (which he turned down).

The point is, when the head clears of extraneous thoughts everyone plays at their peak, given their level of skills and abilities. This is equally true for sports, music, art, writing and everything else. Oh, and it's true in parenting, too.

* * *

One day out of nowhere I received this email from a colleague named Tom Walther:

A few days after I read, in *Prevention From the Inside-Out*, of the study comparing students in school who were only taught when their spirits were up with students who were just taught the curriculum, my seventeen year old daughter came home about 10:30 Friday night. She went right to bed because she had to be up early to take the SAT test. She had done okay the first time but was not satisfied with her score, so this was to be a retake and the last before she submitted her college applications. She took a class on taking the test prior to the first, but had done nothing special to prepare for this one. I was about to go to bed at 2:00 a.m. when she came wandering into the living room with a tear-stained, long face.

"I can't sleep and I have to take the SAT in the morning."

We talked for a while and she was thinking she just wouldn't go. I suggested we see how things felt in the morning and we each trundled off to our beds for the night. In the morning she was up and ready but a little glum and low in spirits.

As I was driving to the test site I was thinking: "If she takes the test in this frame of mind it is not going to help. I wonder what I could do to help her cheer up?"

I had an idea.

I asked, "Would you like to do the success at tests technique?"

She said, "Okay."

I told her we would do it when we stopped at a red light. At the red light I asked her to turn her head and face me. She did. I reached over with my palms of both hands open and with my fingertips mushed and wiggled her cheeks.

That was it! She was a bit surprised and started laughing, and we laughed on to the test site. She got out of the car and went cheerfully off to meet her fate.

When the results came in she had aced the essay and improved her test score by 250 points.

A few weeks ago she told me a friend she'd told the story to told my daughter she'd thought about Julia's story while she was retaking the test and [she, too] bettered her previous score by over 100 points.

Thanks for the book. We'll spread it around and see if we can't brighten the future.

I love that story. When children's minds calm down they are at their best. Oh, that goes for our minds, too.

THE CAPACITY FOR CLARITY AND INSIGHT

Unencumbered by extraneous thoughts we all have this capacity to be at our best and to act out of it. It is built into us.

To see this, all we have to do to is ask ourselves where we are or what we are doing when we get our best ideas.

I have asked many, many people this question. In nearly every case it is when the mind is relaxed. Whether they are in the shower or doing dishes or waking from sleep or taking a walk or knitting or driving or meditating or on vacation or whatever, their minds are relaxed, and into that void pops wisdom. This is true for each of us.

What pops in when the mind is relaxed are insights from a deeper intelligence. This wisdom often takes the form of common sense. We often say to ourselves, "Of course! Why didn't I see that before? It is so obvious."

The reason we didn't see it before is because our minds were filled up, scrambling, processing too much information, pushing our insecurity buttons. We are often too close to something to see the big picture. But if we step back and our head clears it appears. Like a radio receiver when the channel is clear it picks up signals seemingly from out of the blue. The signals it picks up contain an intelligence of fresh ideas.

We would be wise to put this relaxed, flowing thinking into play in dealing with our children.

STEPPING BACK TO SEE WHAT IS REALLY BEING LEARNED

Jasmine, a two year old, was driving her mother, Betsy crazy. Every morning when Betsy needed Jasmine to get ready to leave the house to get to an appointment on time, Jasmine would stall. When her mother went to make her get ready, Jasmine would throw a temper tantrum. Her mother would say, "If you don't come right now, I'm going to leave without you." Jasmine would get scared and cry as her mother grabbed her to get ready.

Betsy, a single mother, is too riled up and frustrated to see her way out of this cycle. Every morning she anticipates the worst and gets it. Every morning she does the most expedient thing at the time. Yet, if she were to pause, take a step back and observe she would see a few things. Betsy would see Jasmine clearly is learning some lessons, only not the lessons her mother wants her to learn.

What lessons is Jasmine learning?

First, she is learning that if someone scares you enough or gets really serious, you cooperate; otherwise, why bother? You may as well stall until you get really scared that they're really going to do something.

Jasmine has not learned the second lesson yet, but it is only a matter of time. Soon she will learn her mother is not really serious about leaving her behind; that it is just an idle threat not to be taken seriously. So Jasmine doesn't really need to listen after all. Further, by her mother lying to her, Jasmine will also learn it is okay to lie; that what's okay for her mother is okay for her.

Jasmine is also learning that power and force ultimately prevail. She is engaged in a battle of wills. Both are immersed in a power struggle. Her mother wins eventually because she is more powerful. But it is only a matter of time—maybe ten or thirteen more years—before the tables are turned.

Seeing this comes from taking the time to step back and ask, *"What is my child learning from what I'm saying and doing?"* Then, common sense steps in. It makes sense to then ask, *"Okay, what do I want my child to learn instead?"*

Disengaged from the struggle answers come to mind, such as, "I'd rather not have my child learn fear from me. I'd rather have her learn she's safe with me." It would be best, then, not to coerce her with fear. If she stepped back even further Betsy would have realized that because the State took Jasmine away from her for a few months and shunted her around from one foster home to another, Jasmine is scared to death about being left behind again. By saying, "I'll leave you if you don't come now," it only exacerbates her fears.

"I'd like my child to be able to count on me and what I say." It would be best, then, to follow through with what is said. If I say I'm going to leave her behind I really have to be willing to do it. Am I willing to really leave her? No! It would be best, then, to find something to say that is not a lie.

"I'd rather not have my child learn that the only time she has to obey is when she's forced. I don't want her to learn that life is about power struggles. I'd rather have her learn that life is about cooperation and helping each other out. I'd like her to learn that when a commitment is made you keep it, whether you feel like it at the time or not." It would be best, then, to disengage from the power struggle and show her caring and firmness at the same time.

With this new perspective Betsy could say, "Honey, I really don't like having to do this to you. I know you don't like it and I'm sorry. But mommy has an appointment that she's got to go to, and I can't leave you behind. So you have to come with me now, sweetie."

Due to past history, of course, Jasmine will throw a temper tantrum and scream that she's not going. She's used to it and it gets attention.

"Sweetie, it's not a question of whether you will go. It's how you will go. It's so much nicer for everyone if you come nicely. It's nicer for you and nicer for me. You tell me how you would like to do it. What can I do to help you?"

If she still kicks and screams and moans we would want to make it a non-issue. As much as humanly possible we would want to not respond. As gently as possible, under the circumstances and saying as little as possible we simply do what we have to do to get her ready and not buy into her temporary insanity. This shows her there is no issue; she is simply going to come with us, either kicking and screaming or nicely and cooperatively.

Betsy might be tempted to say, "We'll do something nice together later when we get back," but we have to be careful. First, we must be absolutely certain if we say it we will do it, because we want her to be able to count on us. Second, we don't want her to think that she'll agree to go *only* to get some reward later. On the other hand we do want to do something nice with her later on general principle. So it depends how it feels at the time. Does it feel solid and right?

By stepping back and gaining new perspective we can see what we really want to accomplish in the long run. Then we only have to do what makes sense because it is only common sense. With a clear mind, wisdom and common sense appear.

HOW DO WE CLEAR OUR MIND IF WE DON'T HAVE A CLEAR MIND?

I knew you were going to ask that.

But it is not about going out of our way to clear our minds. That's too hard. Besides, *trying* to have a clear mind tends to get in the way of having a clear mind. Instead, it is about recognizing that when our head clears, wisdom appears. Simply stopping and taking a step back from the situation or from our child allows for this possibility. If we realize this and see its importance a calm mind will have more of a tendency to appear naturally.

When we feel the need to discipline a child the best thing that can happen is for our wisdom and common sense to interact with their common sense. This happens best when both sets of minds are clear.

When we are relaxed, clear, calm and have nothing on our minds the human mind naturally functions in a healthy way. Having concerns on our minds takes us away from healthy functioning. If what our child is doing is yielding thoughts of concern we could take that thinking in stride and not let it bring us down, because that will lower our spirits. When spirits are low we do not think well because we do not have access to our wisdom at those moments.

Backing off, taking a breather and regaining our bearings sets us up to be more in touch with what our wisdom tells us about what to do. It also helps our children to be more relaxed so they can be more in touch with their own.

TIME OUT?

One common way parents learn to help children calm down is by having them take "time out"; meaning, separate the child from the situation until he regains his bearings. However, many parents use timeout as punishment, relegating the child to a chair or bed or room for sometimes a half hour or more. They say, "If you don't do what I say, you go to time out!"

While this is certainly better than smacking a kid, it is really an inappropriate use of time out. Timeout is only for as long as it takes a child to calm down and regain her bearings. When she has calmed down and can deal with people reasonably again, she can return because she now has her wits about her again. Saying something like, "Sweetie, you'll have to take time out for yourself until you calm down, then we'd love you to come back when you're ready," would be a very appropriate statement.

WISDOM AND COMMON SENSE

Every parent has the wisdom to be a great parent. It is built into us.

When parents can see their children's ability to access their own innate wisdom and treat them as if they have it, those parents will see it emerge in their children.

With innate health and wisdom comes automatic self-respect, respect for others and unconditional self-esteem. When children feel these they naturally will function in a healthy, responsible way, because that's who they really are inside.

Do we have to go out of our way to build this capacity in a child? No! Deep within their spiritual essence or innate health children are naturally inclined toward feelings of self-esteem, positive motivation and respect. They have a natural capacity to understand the natural consequences of their behavior.

This capacity exists prior to children learning any beliefs about what they need. If these natural tendencies are allowed to develop without unnecessary interference, anxiety or pressure they will develop to their full potential of whatever unique talents and abilities they possess. Only when children have been programmed with insecure, self-conscious thoughts do they make unhealthy or inappropriate or destructive decisions—unless they simply do not understand something [more on this in Chapter VIII].

FAITH AND TRUST

Every parent has a deeper consciousness, a deeper intelligence that allows us to know what is best to do in any given situation with our children. We're often just too caught up to see it. Or, we doubt that we have this capacity—we don't trust that we have it.

Being caught up and not having faith and trust in it can only be created from our own thinking. We could have the same faith and trust that our child's innate health and wisdom is there as we have faith and trust that the sun is behind the clouds, even in a blizzard, hurricane or tornado. No one has to convince us. We know when the clouds pass it will be there for all to see and experience, because it never went anywhere in the first place.

FROM A DISTANCE

The reason Carrie Mae (the woman who stormed over to the school with belt in hand in Chapter IV) knew how to approach her son after she calmed down was not because she had learned parenting techniques; rather, it was because from a clear head she knew what to do (although the understanding of moods she'd gained had allowed it to percolate within her).

This calming down happens through disengaging, backing off, observing the situation from a distance. When we do this we will usually know what to do. And even if we don't, our attitudes and feeling will be right so we won't go too far wrong.

If we make the wrong decision because our heads were not as clear as we thought, we can always regroup, apologize after the fact that we blew it and get back on the right track.

Our children get caught up just as we do. *The more we can give them some breathing space to step back and allow what they might do differently to occur to them, the better off they (and we) will be.*

When we pressure children, yell at them, tell them we don't trust them, take over for them, we do not give them a chance to engage their common sense. They are too busy scrambling and running for cover.

HEALTHY MENTAL FUNCTIONING

Hardly a day goes by that we don't experience this healthy state for at least a moment, but it is so natural we don't notice. We don't notice our insights come from the quiet.

In summary, then, the first helpful thing is to know it's there and trust it.

The second helpful thing is to recognize that when we have unhelpful (to us) feelings, if we disengage, back off and observe from a distance we can get ourselves back on track.

Suppose we come home from work tired and our child wants to play. She keeps at us because she wants attention from not being around us all day. Here we have two choices: We could spend time with the child right then, or we could say, "Ohhh, honey, I want to play with you, but I'm really tired right now and if you just give me a little time to myself to take a break for maybe ten or twenty minutes (depending on the child's age), then we'll do something special together." Which would serve us better?

In the first approach we would likely be with the child begrudgingly, and she would feel it. In the second we would be much more present because we took the time to rejuvenate. If it is a very young child we might have to stay in the same room while we rest. If the child keeps bugging us we may have to show them where the hands on the clock will have to be and tell them the hands will move a lot faster if they play by themselves for a while and forget about the clock—and then don't react.

Children don't want to be in conflict any more than we do. If we dropped out of the conflict—if we detached from it—and observed the conflict from a distance we would know better how to resolve that conflict. We would be better able to approach the child again with a feeling of love and access to our wisdom. When the emotions of the moment die down a bit and people take a step back they then tend to see things in a different light. Their state of mind shifts to a higher level of consciousness. Then, together, in a nonthreatening atmosphere, we are all better equipped to work out solutions.

RAPPORT

Once we disengage and have access to our wisdom it would be nice if that wisdom could be communicated. The pathway for this communication is rapport.

Rapport is little more than what we talked about in Chapter I. It means a feeling of closeness. Rapport is a feeling of understanding for our child. Rapport is the path to drawing out the best in our children.

The more rapport we both feel, the more our children will come to us with their concerns. The more rapport we feel, the more they will confide in us. If they feel guilt-tripped by us, we lose rapport. If they feel put down, we lose rapport. If they are afraid of our reaction, we lose rapport. If they're afraid we won't understand and will just come down hard on them, we lose rapport.

Little children are always naturally coming to us to tell us things. This is what they want to be able to continue to do even as they get older. They want to discuss things with us. They only lose the desire when we lose rapport.

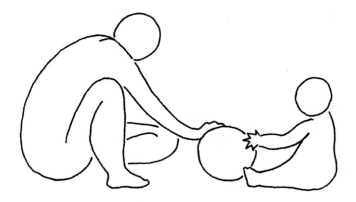

The degree of closeness we feel in the moment is the potential we have for influencing our children positively in that moment. With rapport our children listen to us better. With rapport our kids think (and therefore feel and act) better around us.

Dr. George Pransky says the secret to rapport is being committed to "happy endings." This does not mean letting children have their way or getting our way. It means we both need to be reasonably satisfied with the result. It means within the right feeling we are committed to working it through to resolution no matter how long it takes, and we both feel okay about what happens. We may not be able to agree on everything; that's understandable. On some issues we might have to agree to disagree if we can't get anywhere. However, if we truly commit ourselves to satisfaction and a feeling of resolve on both sides and hang in until it happens, it can be achieved. When both we and our children walk away from nearly every interaction feeling okay, rapport stays high.

Rapport is the foundation for listening (Chapter VII). It is the pathway to teaching (Chapter VIII) and discipline (Chapter IX).

VII. DEEP LISTENING

A child in Judy's daycare center and one of her staff suddenly were not getting along. At the end of the day she needed to have an important discussion with both of them. She asked our daughter to help out during the discussion by watching the child's younger brother. Jaime willingly agreed.

Jaime then received a phone call from a friend inviting her to dinner. She wanted to go badly. Judy said her discussion would last for about ten minutes.

Ten minutes passed. Jaime came downstairs to see if she could go, but Judy was still engaged in heavy conversation and said they needed more time. Jaime went back upstairs. She came down again after another five minutes to an even heavier conversation.

Judy said, "Jaime, it's going to take me another minute. Then I'll drive you over there when I'm finished."

Getting irritated, Jaime said, "Well, can I walk then?"

Judy said, "You can walk if you want, but it's going to take me another minute."

After the heavy conversation ended Judy went upstairs to find Jaime gone. The child had been left alone.

When Jaime came back in a few hours from her dinner Judy landed on her: "How could you have left the child alone? I asked you to do me a favor and you agreed. That's irresponsible!"

Jaime said, "What do you mean? You asked me to watch the kid for ten minutes, and I did. You told me I could walk, so I did."

"The kid could have gotten hurt left alone! I told you I'd be another minute."

"But you told me I could walk. I didn't know it was so important about this kid."

"That's not true, Jaime! I told you!"

71

Heads butted. Both became increasingly frustrated.

I am almost embarrassed to say that, again, I was listening to all this and, again, because I was not the one caught up in the emotions of the moment I heard something.

I said, "Hold on a moment. I think the two of you had two different perceptions of the situation. Then you each acted based on your different perceptions."

Jaime said she thought that was right, but she was still riled up.

In my kindest voice I said, "Jaime, do you see any grain of truth to what your mother is saying?"

"Yes."

"What is it?"

"That I shouldn't have run out on this kid without making sure it was okay, because he could have gotten hurt."

I turned to Judy. "Do you see a grain of truth in what Jaime is saying?"

"Yes, that when I said she could walk, she thought that meant she was free to go."

There is always a grain of truth in the other side. But how would we ever know unless we truly listened to that other side?

The other person's side makes perfect sense to her or him. Both sides are logical, based on the way each person sees it. In the instance above, neither could see the other side, not only because they were too caught up to see the other's logic but because they were not listening to each other. They were too busy defending their own positions. In truth, most of the time we all tend to want to defend our own positions. We do this instead of listening, far more than we realize.

KNOWING HOW TO RESPOND

In the previous chapter we learned to disengage so our minds could clear, to allow access to our wisdom and to be sure our rapport is right. Does this mean we are now ready to take action?

No! Before we act or say anything we have one more task: *to listen deeply!* This step is essential. Yet, of all parenting tasks, listening to our own children is probably the one we are worst at.

First, by truly listening with undivided attention children can feel we care about them and take them seriously. This is not news.

The real purpose of listening to our children in any situation is so we know how to best respond to them.

Read that again.

How would we know the best thing to do, how would we know what to teach them, if we do not understand everything we need to know about what is making them act the way they are?

Suppose when our children do something wrong our first, usual response is to yell, they will run for cover to protect themselves. If our first, usual response is to nag, they will tune us out. If our first response is to listen deeply, they become more attentive and responsive. Which would we rather have?

Since most of us are not used to listening at a deep level, this may take further explanation.

THE ESSENCE OF DEEP LISTENING

Before your baby could talk, how did you know what s/he wanted?

But you did! Maybe not all the time, but most of the time.

If you have a pet, how do you know what it wants? Same thing! You are listening at a level beyond any words. This is the level of deep listening I am talking about. It is picking up the energy between us in a way we know what is truly trying to be communicated. How it works is a mystery. But it happens.

Then when our kids learn to talk we forget all about this most natural way to listen, because we start listening to their words. But we never lose this ability to listen deeply at this level. We simply need a very quiet mind to "do" it. I take that back. There is no "doing." There is only allowing the mind to sink into relaxation with nothing on our minds, with an empty mind. Then our senses are attuned to pick up what someone is *really* trying to communicate beyond or behind their words, much like that radio receiver I described in the introduction.

LISTENING FOR WHAT?

Okay, so paying too much attention to their words may keep us from hearing what we really need to hear. So what do we want to listen for? Essentially, three things:

1. for what they are really trying to be communicated behind the words or actions

2. for how the child makes sense of her or his world and, if necessary, for the grain of truth in what s/he is saying;

3. for what specific thinking (that the child doesn't see or understand) is keeping the child stuck or upset.

Let's explore each of these in more detail.

1. What is our child really trying to communicate beyond the words?

One way to grasp this is if children were unable to use words, what would they be trying to say to us? As implied above it does not take long for even new parents to learn that different types of infant cries mean completely different things. This is listening beyond words, for there are no words to fall back on. Instead of what the words say, what children are really trying to say is far more important and interesting.

When my daughter, Jaime, said to me, "You don't understand kids!" [Chapter 1], those were her words, but what was she really trying to say? "If you want me to respond well, you have to show me love first. You have to say it with love."

Why didn't she just come out and say it then?

She didn't know how! It was buried too far back in her consciousness. She didn't have the words to express it. If she knew how to say it, she would have.

To relate to this better, try to describe "being in love" to someone who has never been in love before. What

75

would you say to them? You've got the words, right? It is not so easy. Or try to describe the color "red" to someone who is color blind? Or try to describe a spiritual experience to someone, using words. Or, even harder, try to describe the game of baseball to someone from another country who never saw a baseball game before. Sometimes words are simply inadequate. We know a lot more than we can actually express. So it is with kids. If we only listen to the words we will miss a whole lot.

Suppose we assume our children do not have the words to express what they would really like to express to us, would we not have to pay a lot more attention? We would have to find out more. We would have to ask them questions before telling them anything; something like—

"Tell me more about that." or,

"Can you give me an example of what you mean?" or,

"Explain what you mean again so I can understand better."

When we ask such questions our ears are then attuned to what makes sense to them about what they are saying. We could really learn something from what makes sense to them. We could learn more about how they are seeing the situation, which is causing them to react as they did, or behave as they do or feel as they do. If we truly, deeply listened to them we might even have an insight about something they said that never occurred to us before. If we are too busy being "right" or "the authority" or defending our positions we will never hear it. This brings us to the second point.

2. How does the child makes sense of his or her world? What is the grain of truth in what s/he is saying?

Not only do we want to know what lies behind our children's words, we also want to know the truth of it to her. We want to be able to see her "truth" as she sees it.

An example of what I mean can be found in the story beginning this chapter when I asked Jaime and Judy if they saw any grain of truth in what the other was saying. Everyone has their own "truth" based on how they see the world. If we listen closely we can hear it.

Given that each child sees each situation in a unique way that makes perfect sense to her, our job as listener is to see it as she sees it. We want to keep inquiring until we are struck by something like, "Oh, I see how she could have come to that conclusion," or, "Oh, I can relate to his logic here!"

The mother from the Modello housing project who asked her son, with a nice feeling, how it made sense to him to pull a knife on a kid at school or to bring a knife in the first place is a good example. We really want to know how in the world this made sense to him. But it did make sense to him—from his perspective! He was really scared. Stuff was going on at that school that we didn't know. "Oh, okay, I get it now!" That does not make it right. It just makes me understand.

"Okay, I can see why you did that now. Now let's talk about how there might be other ways to deal with a situation like that that wouldn't get you into trouble."

Now we can have that conversation. But how could we ever have that conversation without first listening deeply to understand how he made sense of his world to do something like that?

To hear the grain of truth we cannot carry any preconceptions because we will only be listening to ourselves.

LISTENING FOR UNDERSTANDING I

I sat next to a young woman on an airplane. We began talking. She was a very intelligent student who had jumped right from college to graduate school and had not yet been out in the "real world." After a while she began talking about a then new book by Naomi Wolfe that presented an alternative view of feminism, which apparently made her furious.

Innocently I asked if she had read the book. She said, "No," then became silent.

After a few moments she said, "I'll bet you think I'm pretty narrow-minded, to be saying those things without having read the book."

Not being a fool I decided to keep my mouth shut.

Then she said, "Sometimes I think that if you're too open-minded the stuff you know leaks out of your head like a sieve, so it's not good to be too open-minded."

I looked at her, puzzled. Was she joking or serious? By the look on her face I could tell she was trying to make light of it, but deep down she was quite serious. That was pretty much the end of the conversation because I couldn't fathom her view.

The next morning, as I was taking a morning run, something popped into my head that made me realize what she was talking about. Here was a young woman with a head full of ideas. For some reason those ideas defined her life, defined who she considered herself to be. For some reason she desperately needed the world to make sense to her and when it was challenged she felt lost, she no longer knew who she was so she desperately had to cling to what she knew. I don't know why I knew this, but I was absolutely certain of it.

Certainly that was a deeper level of listening than I had enjoyed when talking with her. At the time I couldn't hear it because I was too caught up in the content of what she was saying and whether I agreed or disagreed. When my head cleared, when I wasn't even thinking about it, it occurred to me what her world was like.

I never saw her again, but if I had I could have asked her questions that perhaps would have helped both of us to gain more perspective on her world. I could have asked, "What do you make of the fact that Naomi Wolfe's perspective upsets you so much?" I could have sought out her grain of truth. It would have been a fascinating conversation. All because of deep listening! But so long as I focused on how narrow minded I thought she was, I missed an opportunity to really learn something. I could have gained a deeper understanding. And she could have, too, because she perhaps didn't even know that about herself. And both of us would have had a better time.

A CLEAR MIND

There is only one way to listen for deeper under-standing: Our minds have to be clear and empty so our wisdom can listen instead of it being filtered through our own beliefs.

If we truly want to know what our children do and do not understand about any given situation, our minds must be free from everything we think we know. This is often one of the most difficult things for parents to do. We carry in us what we think is right and wrong, and we tend to filter what we hear through those screens.

Some clarification is in order about what it means to listen with a clear mind. Of course, the mind is almost never completely empty because various thoughts keep popping into it. The question is which of those thoughts are relevant and which are not? Listening with a clear mind really means not being taken in by, or not being caught in, thoughts that are not relevant to our understanding. The thoughts came in; they can now be allowed to pass right on out like a cloud across the sky.

For example, when my son was yapping at me for not driving as well as he thought he could, I first had the thought, "I can't believe he's getting on my case about driving when I'm trying to figure out where I'm going and he's not taking any responsibility for it!" My mistake was taking that thought seriously, taking it to heart, when I should have dismissed it as irrelevant to my understanding. Next I had the thought, "I'm being insulted. I'm offended!" The downward thinking spiral had begun. Instead of taking it and running with it I could have simply allowed it to pass through.

Had I done so, my mind would have had room for a brand new thought. With my wits about me I might have thought, "Gee, what he's doing doesn't really make sense; what is he really trying to say here?" I might have stepped back and reflected upon why he was doing this at this moment. "What is going on with him?" With a clearer head another thought may have popped in: "Well, he's going to be going off to college; maybe he's really insecure about it and taking it out on me." Now, that thought sounds interesting! I would not want to dismiss that thought yet. I would want to put that one on the back burner of my mind and explore it a little more, perhaps ask him some questions about it. Then another thought might pop in: "Maybe he's in too low a mood right now to answer any questions." Another thought worth considering! Then I get another: "But damn it, he has no right to insult me! I can't let him get away with that!" Now that one sounds familiar, suspiciously like what happens when I'm running scared. I can let that one pass.

The above is an example of not allowing contaminating thoughts to take hold and grip us, which keeps our minds as clear as possible. All it takes is awareness of which thoughts aid understanding (ones that sound fresh and new) and which do not (ones that sound like old, familiar news and don't give a great feeling). We want to consider the latter as irrelevant as we would naturally dismiss a thought during this conversation such as, "I wonder what I need to buy at the store today?"

LISTENING FOR UNDERSTANDING II

In short, what we really want to be listening for is understanding, and we can't hear it when anything else is on our minds. It helps to be in a state of puzzlement with our children (and others) until what our child did or said makes sense to us from his perspective. We want to listen and allow other thoughts to pass and, if need be, ask questions with the right feeling until we have a deep grasp of the true message behind all the garbage, until we get to the very bottom of what our child is trying to say.

For example, if our child is lying about something we want to listen and ask questions until we understand how it made sense to him to think he has to lie, and what made him think lying would work? See, there is even a grain of truth—for him—in a lie. Lest anyone conclude from this that I am suggesting to go along with or agree with whatever the kid came up with—not so! Just because we understand does not mean we have to agree. Yet, understanding must come first; any agreement or disagreement can come later. Most often we agree or disagree first and never get to the understanding, and miss what we need to hear to guide us in what to do.

Let's go back to the example in Chapter I when Judy and Jaime got into that "fight." At first Judy heard, "Jaime doesn't care about me enough to clean up, knowing how tired I am when I come home from work." Later in the conversation she heard, "It's a power issue; I'm taking her power away from her." From my greater distance causing my clearer mind at the time I heard, "She's not feeling enough love from us." Same words, different listening, different understandings, different points from which to build communication and subsequent action.

If lecturing turns kids off, asking the right questions at the right time with the right feeling—and by that I mean sincerely wanting to understand, without judgment—opens them up (remember, our feelings tell us when the right time is). The listener will then pick up on our respect—because we are truly trying to understand—and she will respond accordingly. The tone will come out right if our hearts are in the right place, which will occur automatically if we sincerely want to understand.

LISTENING TO SPAWN INSIGHT

At best we want to engage listening that draws our children out of their own typical ways of thinking and enables them to have new insights. If we see something we don't think they understand it may be worthwhile to ask questions (again, if the feeling is right) that might help them see something new. It would be a wonderful thing if they were to see something they never saw before that draws them into a zone of deeper exploration.

Only one thing usually gets in the way of our hearing what we need to hear: our own judgments or opinions. They interfere. They fill our heads and block out understanding. In turn, these become what our kids hear from us. By contrast, as deep listeners, we want everything out of our minds except a question, "What is this person trying to get across to me?" And even that question, once we ask it of ourselves, we want out of our minds. We have set the intention; now we want an empty mind so we can hear the answer from our wisdom. All extraneous debris needs to be cleared away. We then feel closer because we'll be that much more connected.

Here is an example: Suppose our kid comes home saying, "I hate school."

The most unproductive form of listening is no listening at all, such as when we give a response like, "No you don't. You always say you like school," or worse, "What did you do wrong now!?"

More productive listening might be to ask [something like], "What do you mean, honey? What's troubling you about school?"

If the response is, "I just do!" or "It sucks" or "Nothing!" or "Never mind!" that's a signal we have to inquire further (but now may not be the right time if the feeling isn't right).

We may want to follow up with something like, "Did something bad happen to you at school?"

In the process of inquiring we may find out other kids are bullying him, or a teacher or administrator is yelling at her for what she considers no good reason—or whatever.

"Yeah, I can see how you could hate school at this moment."

The point is, with a good feeling and rapport, we want to help her to become open enough to explore further. Listening from the heart is what got us here. Only then does it make sense to ask further questions to help inspire deeper reflection, such as, "What do you think goes on in someone's mind to make them give other people a hard time?" or "What do you think might be going on with him for him to do that to you?" or "What does it mean to you that he does that?"

Our child may never have thought about things in this way before—he was too busy protecting himself—and the answer may hold possible insights. Or not. At this point it becomes an exploration, an inquiry to find the root of the issue or what lies behind the surface.

Parents are often too quick to try to find solutions without thoroughly listening first.

We, ourselves, may even get insights from this kind of deep listening. Suppose our children made a mess in the house. When George Pransky questioned his own kids about this and deeply listened for the answer he was struck with: "Wow, the reason they make a mess all the time is because of how carefree they are, how much they throw themselves so completely into the moment, and then they just move on to the next moment. Their vitality is really such a wonderful thing." From that perspective George wanted to take a different approach to cleaning up. He decided to build upon their vitality by making a game out of it. They ended up playing detective to discover which things were out of place. It worked! But that was just George. It came from his asking questions and listening at a very deep level.

LISTENING AS A GUIDE TO TEACHING

To summarize the third message we want to listen for:

3. We want to listen for the specific thinking (that s/he doesn't know s/he's having) that is keeping the child stuck or upset.

Listening is the bridge between a having a clear mind and knowing what we need to teach our children at the time. Unless we listen, we do not know exactly what our children really need to learn in any given situation.

Example: Suppose we take our six-year-old shopping and the child sees a toy she wants.

We tell her, "I'm sorry, sweetie, you can't have that. It belongs to the store."

Suddenly she throws a temper tantrum. We feel all eyes upon us. We have all witnessed similar scenes and have seen a variety of parental reactions, such as yelling, smacking, yanking the kid bodily out of the store, putting up with the screaming with a pained expression on one's face. At this point most of us tend to listen to our own embarrassment. We only want the kid to shut up and not embarrass us. We react accordingly.

If we were to set aside our own embarrassment, take a step back and truly listen, we might see that our own embarrassment isn't the most important issue, that what is going on is merely a symptom of larger issues. If we listened deeply, what are some of the things we might hear?

We might hear that the problem is really that our child's state of mind is off. What does a child need when her state of mind is off? Love and understanding!

We might hear the larger issue is our child doesn't understand how to keep from getting out of control and how to keep her bearings when things aren't going her way. This then becomes what we need to teach.

We might hear that the child's expectations, before she went into the store, were unrealistic. This may mean we need to better prepare her before we walk into a store filled with things she's probably going to want.

Whatever we hear from deep listening helps us know specifically what we need to teach.

Example: Suppose we ask our twelve year old to clean the living room. We come back to find papers and books and coats scattered everywhere.

Our usual thought might be, "He didn't do what I told him!" We might attribute his actions to any number of motivations and land on him for whichever we believe true.

Or, we could truly listen. For example, we could ask ourselves, "Does my child really understand what 'clean' means, or am I just assuming he sees it as I do?"

Hmm.

To find out, I may need to ask some questions [something like]: "Buddy, when I say 'clean the living room, what does that mean to you?"

"Put my toy away."

We look around and we see he in fact did put away the toy he most recently played with. Oh.

"Well, Bud, now that I know what you think I meant by clean, I can see you did a great job of that. Just so you know, when I say clean here's what I mean…"

Before, we didn't take into consideration that he doesn't see "clean" the way we see "clean." So we have to help him understand. This is the opposite of getting on his case for not cleaning up the way we want him to.

Example: Suppose we tell our fifteen year old that she can't go to a party, and she slams the door in frustration. Not listening well, we might get on her for slamming the door or remind her who is boss and what we say, goes, and we don't want to hear any complaints.

Or, we could step back and listen. Again, we could ask ourselves some questions.

Does she really understand what our decision is based on, or why we care about it so much?

Might our decision not make sense to her because she doesn't understand the situation as we see it? Does she have any idea what all the factors were that we took into consideration? "Wait a minute, how did I arrive at this decision? Am I clear, myself, about why I don't like the idea?"

Oops.

Before we check to see if it makes sense to her, we'd better be sure it makes sense to us. What are the reasons we decided this? If we don't have a sound reason we may even reach a different conclusion. Through our listening we might see the reason she's rebelling is because we are not working out decisions like this as a team so everyone has the same understanding.

Suppose we believe that our kids go out of their way to give us a hard time. If we really listened we would likely find this is the case only in the rarest of instances—almost never. Before we jump to that conclusion it would be best to listen first and give our kids the benefit of the doubt. Listen for any insecurity. Listen for any distress. Listen for what they don't understand.

In sum, truly listening will guide us in the direction of what is really going on and about what we need to teach.

QUESTIONS THAT AID LISTENING

Here are examples of the types of questions that may help us to listen better. Please understand, I am not suggesting these as pat questions. I am only giving examples of the types of questions that might help us see more deeply.

The first type of question is not really a question. It is not something we ask of the other person. It is what we ask of ourselves in preparation for listening. With questions like this, we set our intention to hear the answers, and once we ask we then clear our minds and reflect so we can hear wisdom speak:

- I'd like to get touched by how he sees his world.
- I'd like to understand what makes sense to her about this.
- I'd like to see what he sees that I don't.

- I'd like to understand what she is trying to get across to me.
- I'd like to understand what he is not seeing that would help him.
- I'd like to see what she doesn't realize.

Now that our minds are prepared, during the conversation to aid our understanding we might ask questions something like these:

- Can you help me understand this better?
- Tell me more. Can you say it in another way?
- Do you mean _____?
- What do you make of this?
- What does this mean to you?

Questions such as these draw the talker into a zone of deeper reflection and, hopefully, understanding. Don't forget, we want to listen until we have a healthy respect for how our child sees things and therefore we want to get our own judgments, opinions and disagreements out of the way as much as possible.

Oh, it might also be worthwhile to use the type of listening recommended in this chapter on your partner or spouse (but you can pretend I didn't say that because this is a parenting book).

Everything this book has been pointing to is an understanding of life from a perspective that at first sounds strange. In a nutshell, it is about how the interplay of *three principles* creates the experience we have of life, including the experience we have of our children. The three principles are: 1) *Universal Mind* (the life force, the energy behind all life, the intelligence behind life, the source of life itself); 2) *Thought* (the power to create); 3) *Consciousness* (the power to experience life, and the ability to be aware of what our thoughts create).

The way it works is that some unfathomable source gives us two powers or abilities to create how we see life and therefore how we experience it, to create and experience how we see each and every thing that happens to us, including how we see ourselves and how we see our children. Out of what we see, we then think, feel, and act accordingly.

Anything that happens to us in life, any situation or circumstance we happen to find ourselves in, any person we happen to encounter, everything our children do, every aspect of life gets filtered through these three principles to give us our experience of those things. We can have no pure or direct experience of anything that happens in the outside world. It is always filtered through Mind, Consciousness and Thought. In other words, we use our creative power of thought to make it all up—not on purpose, but we do—and our power of consciousness gives us a 'real" experience of whatever we've made up. It is a perfect system.

When we encounter something our child does, we can experience the same child and the same event at an unfathomable number of different levels. For example, if we get a thought of anger, the anger feels very real. But given the same situation, if we happen to get a thought of compassion, the compassion feels just as real. And nothing about the situation has changed. We've inadvertently made up how we see it and therefore what we feel.

In short, we make up how our kids looks to us. We make up how we take what they do. And then we really feel whatever we've made up because our consciousness takes our thinking and turns it into the feeling we get. No one can talk us out of this reality—unless and until our thinking changes.

Of course things happen to us in life over which we seem to have little or no control, but we are capable of experiencing these events and circumstances *only* through our thoughts entering our consciousness and giving us a "real" experience. We may not even be aware of what we're thinking, but we are having those hidden thoughts just the same. Thus, when we think this is "the way it really is," for everyone "the way it really is" differs, and "the way it really is" even differs for us at different times depending on our moods.

The implications are enormous and profound. Ultimately, all we can experience is within us. And we get to decide how seriously we take what we see.

Most of us tend to look to the external world to provide answers, or to blame. We think our parenting problems are caused by our kids, when they are really caused by the way we are seeing our kids. When we see our children in a different light, and act accordingly, new worlds of possibilities unfold before us.

Note: This understanding was first *seen* by a man named Sydney Banks (now deceased) in a moment of profound epiphany. Then Drs. George Pransky and Roger Mills (also now deceased) turned what Banks saw into a new psychology. Both applied this understanding as an approach to parenting and to many other fields.

VIII. TEACHING KIDS WHAT THEY NEED TO LEARN

What is the most important thing we can teach our children?

It is probably for children to know how to engage their own wisdom and common sense so they know what makes the most sense to do in any given situation. This might be called "self-reliance."

The pathway to self-reliance is through the heart. Just as we want to deal with our own children most effectively by stepping back and engaging our wisdom, so we want our children to be able to do the same to know how best to deal with whatever difficulties might arise in their own lives. Besides helping them learn everything this book has been pointing to about know how to step back, clear their head or quiet their mind to engage their wisdom, we can also help our children gain self-reliance by *teaching them what we take into account in reaching our conclusions,* instead of laying our conclusions on them.

PREPARATION FOR TEACHING

It is wise to remind ourselves again and again that, to teach our children anything, they will hear and react to the quality of our feeling, not to our words. If they hear us being judgmental they will only hear the judgments and will shrink away. If they hear and feel love and understanding they will expand and open to what comes next. To expect our teaching to take hold our hearts must be in the right place.

Remember, too, that teaching works best when it arises out of listening. Through listening we hear what our children need to learn at any given time. Otherwise our teaching may be off base. If we don't listen deeply, even

93

our best teaching will not make a particle of difference, for they won't be ready to hear it.

Although children always have wisdom within them they often do not know how to engage or access it. Also, they are not born with knowledge about the situations they will encounter in life and what to do about them. They are not born with skills. All these they have to acquire and learn.

THE TEACHING PROCESS

How can we prepare the child's mind to take in new learning? How will the child be most open to listening to us the way we want to listen to him? It is most helpful to:

- create a warm, loving, caring supportive environment in which learning can best occur
- model the behavior we want to see in them through our own actions
- help the child gain an understanding of the issue we want her to learn about
- if needed, allow the child opportunities to experience the natural results of his behavior

TEACHING RESPONSIBILITY

As an example, let's see how this might play out in trying to teach our children responsibility. Perhaps more than anything else, most parents want their kids to be responsible. How do we teach children responsibility?

Responsibility is both an understanding and a skill. It is not something a child brings naturally into the world. Yet, all children are born with the capacity (barring a very few organic difficulties) to become responsible. Thus, we need to draw this capability out of them and teach a few things along the way.

As implied by the four bullets above, responsibility is best learned in four ways:

1. through creating the right environment for learning

This means bringing to life everything stated in the previous chapters of this book.

2. by modeling responsible behavior through our own actions

What we show them is usually what we get. Actions speak far louder than words. They watch us very carefully, They don't do what we say as much as they do what we do. So if we want our children to be responsible we would be wise ourselves to model responsible behavior.

3. by helping the child gain an understanding of "responsibility"

Essentially, we want to take opportunities—in a calm, loving, caring way, when emotions are not charged but when something occurs that reminds us of responsibility—to discuss with our children what responsibility is, what it means, why it's important, what would happen if people were not responsible, and the effect being responsible or not has on others.

4. by allowing the child to experience how responsible and irresponsible actions effect one's life

A mistake often made by parents is to rely on consequences to teach. The problem is, consequences come after the fact of the behavior. *Long before consequences enter the picture comes understanding.* In this chapter we concentrate on helping children gain the understanding. How do we help our children understand how their actions affect others? How do we help them know what responsible action is and what it isn't? This is where the goodies really lie, because if kids truly understand responsibility and all its ramifications, more often than not they will act responsibly and we'll never need to resort to consequences. So it is best to look for nonthreatening opportunities to help them understand it.

As examples, let's look at this developmentally.

From ages 6 to about 11 children are at the stage where they can both grasp concepts and are most open to learning and listening to their parents. So while watching TV together, if we see someone being irresponsible we can ask our child what effect she thinks that character's behavior is having on others. We can ask if she thinks that behavior was responsible and why. We can ask how being responsible plays out in her own life. We can ask her whether she thinks that certain of her classmates and friends are responsible or not, and how can she tell? Later, if we see her engaging in irresponsible behavior we can remind her of our conversation so she can connect it to what she is doing in the moment. If we want responsibility developed we must be committed to ensuring she gains this understanding.

This takes patience. We can't expect our children to get "responsibility" all at once. We probably didn't! All we have to do is bring to mind some of our behaviors when we were young to realize it took us a while to understand responsibility.

In other words, to help our kids understand responsibility we need to:

- be creative in helping them understand it, such as looking around for examples in ourselves, in others and in themselves
- be committed to their learning it
- be patient while they learn it.

The world presents infinite opportunities for creative learning. As examples, together we could learn more about how behaviors affect others. We might even make a game of it, pretending we're private investigators observing whether we think others are being responsible or not. We might observe how the differences in behaviors affect others. We could ask our children to contrast how they are affected when we (parents) deal with them in different ways. We could ask them to think of a time when we did something that affected them and whether they considered what we did to be responsible. We might be surprised at their answer. Then we could discuss other ways it might have been handled in a more responsible way.

From ages (about) 12 to 18 it's almost like teenagers forget everything we thought they knew. One way to teach responsibility at this age is to trade "freedom" for "responsibility." In other words, we're willing to give him all the freedom he would like *if* we are absolutely certain he is going to use that freedom wisely and responsibly. He'll prove that by his actions. It's completely up to him. [More on this later.]

BACK TO SELF-RELIANCE

At some point our children will go off into the world without us. If they are not self-reliant they will have a very difficult time.

We want to help our children understand the relationship between what they are doing, what their choices are, and their own internal satisfaction and fulfillment. We want them to be able to look at a situation, see what is in their own long-term best interests and act accordingly.

Suppose our teaching does not seem to be getting through. Chances are one of three things is amiss: 1) our rapport has dropped; 2) we're in an unproductive frame of mind; 3) we don't know what we're talking about.

Sometimes we are too quick to try to teach. We have a lot to teach our kids—from how to use a fork, to how to cross a street, to how to clean a room, to how to be responsible, to how to drive, to how to deal with peer pressure, to how to avoid drugs. I know this is repetitious but it bears repeating again and again because it is so important: No matter what we try to teach—no matter what we say—it is not going to be taken in, understood, accepted, taken to heart, if we don't communicate it from an open, responsive, caring, loving state of mind and we have rapport *in that moment*.

We want to assume our children want to learn. When very young our children thirst for knowledge. They soak it up. This is their natural state. Later, inadvertently, we often take the fun out of learning. Our children do not move fast enough for us; we get upset and take it out on them. We want them to move faster or do it right at the expense of taking the time to help them learn it for themselves. All for expediency! Learning becomes no fun. Then school often reinforces how un-fun learning can be. Sometimes it's even painful. So children lose that natural desire to learn. But it's not as if that natural desire ever really gets lost. It never really disappears because it is still within them. We can see this clearly because whenever something catches their fancy they automatically become interested.

Yes, it may take more time but it will likely save time in the long run.

TEACHING SELF-RELIANCE THROUGH TAKING CARE OF THE HOUSEHOLD

When children act in unfathomable ways (to us) it may be because they simply have not learned all there is to know about a given situation. Consider the issue of helping out around the house, often the bane of parents' existence. Are our kids good-for-nothing-lazy bums, or have they not understood how cleaning is in their best interests? If they understood how cleaning is in their own best interests they would naturally develop self-reliance around cleaning. Once it takes hold in their own minds we would not have to be on their backs about cleaning up again because they would be doing it for themselves.

The more children understand with their own internal logic the need for household chores and why they are important, the more likely they will do them without a struggle. If children can see household chores as fun, the more likely they will do them. This may seem like a great leap, but one key is how we parents present and teach household responsibilities, determined by how we see them ourselves. If we see them as a chore and drudgery we will pass that on and it becomes what our children pick up. [Ha! I just realized something while writing this: We want our children to pick up their clothes, but they're mostly picking up our own attitude about cleaning up.]

At some point every child wanted to help his parents around the house; meaning, at some point (usually a very young age) our child saw it as fun. He wanted to help sweep the floor or help us cook. This means the desire is inside of them. How did we handle it? Did we inadvertently kill it in them? Did we ruin the fun of it? Did we keep getting on them for not doing something right or for making a mess? Then we wonder how they lost their desire.

It is never too late! We could lighten it up. We could be a team working together. We could have a feeling of camaraderie. How can we make it fun?

We could also try to appeal to their own common sense about the need for cleaning up. Why is it important anyway? Why is it important to us?

But maybe we don't really know why it is important to us. Maybe we think it's the thing to do because our parents told us it was. Is that good enough? Sure, we could probably get compliance by forcing them, but is that really what we want? Forcing them to comply has nothing to do with building self-reliance except take it away. Would it not be more satisfying if they cleaned up because they thought it was the right thing to do for themselves?

Sometimes kids may have to be jump-started. If their room is atrocious it may be too overwhelming for them to clean. We may have to do it once for them (maybe a few times) or do it with them because it is too overwhelming. After that we can decide what we can do together to keep it that way.

Kids usually want to help out if there's a nice feeling about it, but often we're on their case, so it becomes the last thing they're usually interested in.

Also, if we want their rooms clean, is ours clean? If it's not, what's the point to them? They won't understand what the difference is, and for good reason. Remember, they are watching!

Do our children understand that keeping up a household is a big responsibility? Do they understand how much there is to do? Do they understand what it is like to have the work burden fall on one person if others don't share the load or live up to their commitments? Do they understand how much easier it is for everyone to share the load? Do they understand that if they mess something up after you spent hours cleaning they will likely feel the effects of your reaction?

If I come into a room and see that my child has made a mess I night have a tendency to ask, "So who are you leaving that mess for to clean up?" or "Let me get this straight, you're expecting me or your mother to clean that up for you?" I want to keep it lighthearted but still make the point.

If they don't live up to their commitments we could ask for their advice about how we might resolve it. Remember we're talking about entering into a dialogue and partnership here, not badgering them.

Is it important for families to have minimal rules to keep order? We could make this decision for our children, but would they be learning self-reliance? If we make the decision independent of them they are not gaining the benefit of the potential learning inherent in making this decision. If we want them to become self-reliant about rules and following them, they have to see the importance for themselves of rules. Why are rules important? What happens if there aren't rules? What kind of rules are appropriate and which aren't? How do we decide which are important?

Back to the example of keeping a clean house, should there be rules? This is a decision each family needs to make for themselves.

If our children are not keeping the house clean enough for us, we could first step back, observe and listen. We could ask ourselves what our children do not understand about cleaning up. How are they seeing it? What is important to us about cleaning up?

Would they be moved by the idea of helping each other out? Would they be moved by the fact that it takes longer for people to do things alone? If not, what would move them?

When they're young we may have to show them what needs to be cleaned and how to clean it. Even if they're older we may have to show them; they may never have considered what is involved in making something clean to people's satisfaction.

For example, if we want our children to learn table manners we want to teach them the logic. Step back and watch and listen for what they don't understand. They are not born with the knowledge of why table manners are important. We may have to ask ourselves what the logic is of not slurping food; we might not readily know ourselves. If it is not clear for us, how can we expect it to be clear to them? Do they understand that people are affected by what they do? Do they understand that certain people are bothered by certain things, and some people get turned off when they see others eating in a way they would call disgusting? Do they understand that if we live our lives without bothering people our own lives run more smoothly?

The same holds true for keeping rooms clean. What is the logic? Would they be moved by the fact that clothes get wrinkled and ruined? Probably not. They don't often pay for their own clothes. Would it move them to know that cleaning up after oneself keeps the pace of one's life sane? Whoa! A statement like that may or may not affect them, but it is often one that makes people sit up and take notice because it is not something people normally think about when considering reasons for cleaning. It often does something for the mind to enter an orderly room; it makes many people feel peaceful. Take an eight-year-old into museum or an empty church and ask what feeling he gets. Our lives get so fast-paced that cleaning up after ourselves provides automatic regulation to keep the pace of our lives more calm. I had never thought about this before I heard George Pransky say it. I then tested it on my daughter, and Jaime seemed taken aback. She had never thought about it before either. She realized its truth. After that, she seemed to have slightly less aversion to cleaning up after herself. Not that she always did, but she cleaned up more, and when she did it seemed to calm her—provided she did it in the right frame of mind. I am not suggesting this will work for all kids, only that we have to help children find their own logic and reasons that will resonate with them, probably reasons that may surprise them a little.

We can step back and observe what their patterns are. If we ask our children to clean up the living room, and we find papers and books on the floor and their jackets on the couch, perhaps the kids don't see "clean" the way that we see "clean." We have to listen and teach. So we check out what they did:

"What about the papers on the floor?"

"Oh yeah."

"What about the jacket."

"Oh yeah."

They don't see it! How many times have we done the dishes and then our partner comes along and finds some caked-on food left on a dish or glass. We didn't see it, even though we were sure we cleaned it well. That's what happens with kids.

Again we could create a fun game. "I'm going to clean up the room and I want you to tell me what to clean up. Then after I clean up I want you to inspect it." We could even make up inspector sheets. But our hearts have to be in right place.

We might say, "Okay, together, let's find a place for everything and have both of us get into a habit of putting things away. And if I don't put my things away, you tell me, okay?"

* * *

Cynthia Stennis, a parent and former staff social worker from the Homestead Gardens housing project in Florida came up with her own special way of teaching the importance of household chores. She said, "We sit down together and I ask, 'What do you think has to get done? We're all in this together. We need to work out a system. How would you like to contribute?'"

If Cynthia came home from work and found the apartment messy she would say, "This is your house. Do you want it to look like that? Show me how you want your apartment to look."

Sometimes she came home from work and started to go the kitchen to cook but her kids wanted her attention. She was upset because the house was messy (or rather, because of her thinking). But she knew better than to say anything when upset. So she held her tongue until her spirits rose. Then, with a half smile on her face, she said, "You guys wouldn't clean the bathroom, but you want me to listen to you and play with you? And I guess since you're not sleeping in your bed, you want me to make up your bed. And I guess you want me to pick up your shoes, even though they're not my shoes." Cynthia knew the more she made light of it, the more she made it fun, the more they could understand.

Her other options are either: 1) do everything herself to get the house the way she wants it, then get angry because she has to do everything; 2) punish her children for not doing what they're supposed to; or 3) do what many parenting courses suggest, "You can't do what you want until you've done what's expected." This last approach may be okay, but it does not promote cleaning for cleaning's sake because of the power it holds over them.

Cynthia chose the lighthearted-but-still-get-the-point-across approach. In this way her children really understood what the issues were because it was done in a non-threatening, respectful manner. She put the burden of responsibility back on them so they could check out for themselves how they would really feel to be in her shoes. It worked! Her kids became very helpful around the house.

Cynthia did the same with the issue of curfew. Cynthia's then fifteen-year-old son asked, "How late can I stay out?"

"If you had a son fifteen years old, how would you feel? What would you do?"

Again, the issue got put back on him, so it teaches him to consider what is involved.

Suppose after that discussion he still came in late?

Calmly, she says to him, "Look at the time."

He says, "I know, I won't do it again."

"Okay, well what will have to happen when you do? What would you do if it were your son?"

She wants him in the position where, if he were the parent, how would he treat his child.

Not everyone would be comfortable using Cynthia's style; that was her own. Everyone has to find their own style they're comfortable with. The point is, through her questioning her kids came to *understand*, and once they understood they acted accordingly and carried it with them for the rest of their lives..

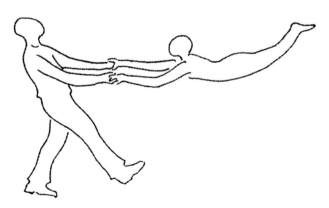

TEACHING SELF RELIANCE THROUGH
DISAPPOINTMENT AND BOREDOM

At a fairly early age one of the things children need to learn is how to deal with disappointment and boredom.

If kids are disappointed about something many of us have a tendency to try to distract them, to get them involved in something else. This is okay occasionally, but what does it teach them? They never have to really reckon with it.

It may be better to let them be disappointed. The fact is there are disappointments in life. Not everything goes the way we'd like it to. If they get disappointed they may cry in frustration, but then it's over and they move on; it's no big deal. Then, later in life when they then experience big disappointments, such as the loss of a love relationship, they may not get bowled over so easily and will be able to move on. If our children are disappointed and crying we can show them compassion about their frustration but we also know, from our own experience, that something else will come around the bend. Disappointments are part of life; they're unfortunate but we get over them. They're not the end of the world and we move on. We might even learn from them. Some people believe everything happens for a reason. Whether it's true or not (and who really knows?) those who believe that do not have a tendency to be crushed by disappointments.

Part of "self-reliance" is children learning to handle their own negative feelings and temporary setbacks.

Many kids get bored. When kids are bored many parents have a tendency to try to relieve them of their boredom, either by directing them into some other activity or telling them to do something to busy themselves. Yet, if we look closely we can see people often are bored because they are too highly stimulated. They are used to running, running, having a million things to do and going on all at once. TV doesn't help, flashing and jumping images so quickly between one thing and the next, keeping that stimulation so high that three seconds without a change begins to seem like an eternity. Then, when it stops, children feel lost. Facebook and texting keep kids even more stimulated, and when it all stops they don't know what to do with themselves; they feel they need something to fill the void. When the stimulation stops for a few moments boredom steps in to take its place.

What if we simply let kids be bored? Boredom is a mind going too fast. Slowing down for a while might do them some good. Once their minds calm down it will occur to them what to do. Slowing down helps us all find our bearings. If we run around trying to find something else to stimulate our children with, they will need more and more stimulation to be happy. A lot of enjoyment can come out of peace and quiet—if we let it. Do we want to be entertaining our kids all the time, or do we want them discovering how to entertain themselves? Of course we want to spend quality time with our children, but we don't want to be stimulating them all the time.

"Mommy, I'm bored!"

"I'm sure you'll find something you want to do eventually."

Part of self-reliance is children learning to take care of their own entertainment. Often, the most beautiful and enjoyable moments are the most peaceful, when we deeply appreciate the little that is going on.

JUDGMENT CALLS

When teenagers want to go somewhere a parent considers dangerous or inappropriate there is no way to tell whether something bad will actually happen. It's a judgment call.

The kid really, really wants to go. It seems like the end of her life if she can't go. We're uncomfortable with the idea. How do we keep the conversation respectful and caring?

"Sweetie, I don't know whether I'm right, but as a parent it's my job to make this decision. Some things are judgment calls. Do you agree that there are some things parents need to make the decision about? I don't know whether I'm right here or not, but in this case I'm not willing to take the chance to let you go."

The kid may not like it. She still may say, "Dad, you don't understand! I need to go!" Or, "Nothing will happen! It's safe!"

"I'm sorry, honey. You may be right. But in this case I'm not willing to take the chance, and here's why…"

I'd better have a darn good reason because if I don't, she's going. But is it a question of potential danger? If it is I may not be willing to take the chance, even if odds are she'll be safe.

The point here is, she's bound to respect it more than my just saying, "No way! Case closed! You can't go, period." So long as the child feels really listened to and understands it's a tough question for a parent and I'm doing my best as a parent to keep my child safe, and she feels a sense of understanding about that, even if she doesn't like it, we will usually end up okay. People can't always reach agreement but, as Dr. Steve Glenn said, they need to feel listened to and taken seriously.

Some parents will ask, "Why should I waste my time? I'm the parent! What I say goes!"

That may be true, but we have to ask ourselves, what do we want our kids to learn?

Will he learn that when someone bigger than you tells you to do something, you do it. Then suppose some big guy comes along wanting to sexually abuse him? Or what happens when he's in a situation where he can tell a smaller kid what to do? What do we really want our kids to learn?

Or, do we want our kids to learn, as a parent what are the kinds of things we consider when we make decisions like this?

Of course there are times when parents have the last word. Yet, if we want our relationships with our children to prosper and for them to learn how decisions are made in life and how to access their own common sense, we want to help them understand as much as possible where we are coming from and how we see it. But, remember, we also want to listen to what they would do and be open enough to be affected by how they see it and to have our minds changed.

The alternative is force of will and bad feelings. Is it worth it to be right all the time and have a bad relationship?

On the other hand, some things are just common sense. Does one go walking alone at night in a neighborhood where people have been known to be hurt, shot, or raped? Okay, even then we don't know something bad is guaranteed to happen, but that's obvious common sense. Kids can understand the difference between common sense and judgment calls.

HOW DO WE KNOW WHAT KIDS NEED TO LEARN?

Kids need to understand how to get along in the world. We can't leave it to chance. How will we know specifically what they need to learn? By watching and listening carefully.

If a kid is having problems with a certain issue, such as being loud when the parent is on the telephone, that becomes our signal for what she needs to learn. Kids need to learn many things we take for granted. If we're too quick to get upset or punish or use logical consequences we've missed an opportunity to help the child learn self-reliance.

So we step back and ask ourselves, "Why would she be acting this way? What doesn't she understand?" Then, we watch and listen with an open, clear mind. We'll usually see what she needs to understand

Back to the example of my kid making noise when I'm on the phone, stepping back, I ask myself, "Why is it important for her not to make noise when I'm on the phone?" What seems obvious may not be. Some things we think are important may not be. Is this a big enough deal for me to make an issue out of? After all, we can't make everything into a huge issue because then the impact of the really huge ones is diminished. So we have to pick our spots. So I ask myself the question and wait for an answer.

Actually, I've got lots of reasons. The most obvious one is when she's making noise I can't hear. It's important for me to hear another person who's talking to me. Noise is distracting. I can't think well. I'm not at my best. I also think it is very important to be able to give someone my undivided attention; it's not respectful not to." Yup. Those are my reasons.

Now that I know what the answer is for myself I ask, "Okay, what doesn't she understand?" Then I step back, watch and listen.

I may find the child has no idea she's even making noise. I may find she understands she's making noise but isn't thinking about anyone else but herself. I may find she doesn't understand that when she's making noise, others can't hear. We say, "Of course she understands this; that's ridiculous!" But does she really? And if she does fully understand it, why is she still making noise? Something doesn't compute. It's puzzling.

Whatever we discover the reason is from our listening, that's what we teach about!

Let's say I discover the answer is that she gets caught up in playing and doesn't even realize she's making noise or bothering others.

"Sweetie, I know you're not doing this on purpose, but here's what it sounds like to me when you do that." Then I may have to demonstrate—in whatever way I come up with—how noise makes it hard for me to hear, so she gets it. I may have her talk on the telephone and I'll make the kind of noise she's making. Or I may have her try to concentrate on something and then make all kinds of noise around her. I just have to be creative. If I do any of that stuff, though, she's got to know I'm not doing it to be mean or that two wrongs make a right; I'm just trying to demonstrate what it's like for her to experience on the other end.

With a nice feeling in my heart I can ask her if she thinks it's important to be able to hear other people when they're talking to her, and I can deeply listen to her response. Then we can have a nice talk about why I think being able to hear someone is important to me.

This is important! Once we hone in on an issue we have to stick with it, one way or another, until we come to a meeting of the minds. Usually that can only happen through open dialogue. This is how learning happens, except if it happens through experiencing natural consequences (meaning, letting the natural course of events unfold and make their point naturally, such as leaving a banana peel on the floor and slipping on it). Still, sometimes we cannot afford to have the natural consequence happen, as in teaching the child why she should not run out in the street.

Most children below age seven are developmentally unable to reason well, so it is not worth expecting they will. At that age we have to take quick action. We can still talk to them about why we're doing what we do, which sets up a pattern and can begin as early as possible, but we can't expect the child to grasp what we're talking about. Still, they pick up the tone and begin to get used to this approach.

Again, the most important thing to develop in children is to be able to draw upon their own wisdom and common sense. Ultimately we're teaching them what we're modeling here: how to step back from a situation so the head clears, we gain more perspective, we see the big picture and have the best chance of knowing what to do. When a child's mind is in a quiet, calm state she will usually find her common sense. The more secure they are, the more access they have to their wisdom.

At the same time we want to both maintain rapport and be sure the child understands we stand behind what we say. We will stick with the issue at hand until it is learned, patiently.

Children are so innocent. They can get out of control and not see how it affects others. They need guidance and support from their parents to teach them how to keep their bearings, how to function when they get out of control, how "out of control" happens. When they lose control it means they're in pain, something is wrong, off-kilter, and they're suffering. We are aiding them by helping them regain their bearings. They don't want to be out of control—it doesn't feel good to them any more than it does to us—but they can't help it. They're doing the only thing they know how to do in that moment. Again, if we take a step back, we can see what specifically needs to be taught, and patiently stick with it.

One caution: *If we stop enjoying our children we're doing too much teaching.*

SUMMARY POINTS ABOUT TEACHING

In summary, to teach our children anything and have it stick, the following ingredients are needed.

- I want to be crystal clear in my own mind why this issue is so important to me.
- I want to be the model of what I want to teach.
- I want to be sure my heart is in the right place. Is my child feeling respect from me? Is my child feeling that I have faith in him, that with understanding I know he'll be able to do what's best? Do I see that my child really wants to learn and wants to be a productive, nice person? If I'm not holding this view in the moment I want to step back and recognize the feelings I'm carrying is what he is picking up. Then I want to use that observation to right myself. Do we have rapport right now?
- I want to ask myself, "In the long run, what will my child be learning through this?"
- I want to understand that the purpose of my guidance is their future self-reliance
- I want to take as many opportunities as I can (without losing enjoyment for my kid) to teach what I see needs teaching, being sure I help her understand the reason why this issue is so important to me.
- I want to step back and observe what specifically it is that he doesn't understand that explains why he is having this difficulty. For example, "Okay, my kid doesn't want to clean off the table. He knows how to do it. He knows we expect it. He's not doing it. What doesn't he understand? What doesn't he get about its importance where it would make sense to him to do that job?" Maybe he doesn't understand that sometimes you have to do things that you don't want to do for the greater good. If I'm stuck and can't see the reason in the moment I want to say to myself, "Right now I can't see what the problem is, but I'd really like to see it." Then I

want to forget about it and keep observing and have faith I will eventually see what he needs.

- I want to reach a meeting of the minds and stay in rapport while doing so.
- I want to stick with it until it is learned

TEACHING RESPECT

To illustrate the above, let's walk through how, as a parent, I would want to teach my own child respect. What process would I go through?

First I ask myself, "Why do I care about respect? Why is respect important to me?"

The reason may be different for each of us. For me, I would say respect is important because it is the essence of people getting along in the world. Without respect we would have disrespect. People then would think they had license to walk all over anyone at any time. People would get hurt. There would be chaos.

Does this explanation satisfy me? Do I feel grounded in it? Pretty much, but it feels like I'm missing something. Respect is also something that one needs for oneself. People who don't have respect for themselves don't care, and when people don't care they tend to harm themselves and others.

This feels closer. Maybe I should look up "respect" in the dictionary to perhaps give me more of an insight.

The American Heritage Dictionary says "to respect" means: "1. to feel or show esteem for, to honor." Wow! That's nice. Respect is the basis for esteem. Respect means honoring people. Imagine how peaceful, how beautiful the world would be if everyone honored everyone else!

What else does it say? "2. to show consideration for; avoid violation of; treat with deference." Again, wouldn't the world be a wonderful place to live if we each took it upon ourselves to be considerate of other human beings and their property and avoided violating them in every way. That's how I would want to live!

What would we have if we didn't have respect? The antonym of respect is, "abuse; misuse; scorn." Which world would we rather live in? I know where I stand. I sure would rather be honored than abused or scorned. If I want that for me, I ought to be willing to give that to others. That goes for my children, too. In fact, it is really important to me that they be that way. I would like them to live in such a world, and it begins at home.

Now I feel very well-grounded in why respect is so important to me, and why I want my children to learn it.

With that solid grounding in the issue next I want to take every opportunity I can find (without being obnoxious about it) to be sure that they learn it.

Most important, I want to be sure I continually show them respect, even when I am angry with them. If I am so caught up in my own thinking or my moods that I blow it and do not show respect I want to go back and apologize. I want to let them know how I realize I was not showing respect and why that was wrong. If I want to teach them respect I want to be the model of it—from their perspective.

For example, if I want them to respect my belongings, to take care of them, to not get into my things, I can't get into their things. If I break something of theirs by accident I'm responsible for replacing it. If they break something of mine, if I yell at them I am not honoring them, so I have to watch myself and, if I slip, apologize. I have to get myself in order first.

Next, to teach respect I want to begin at the earliest possible time, when they are very young, when they are first able to comprehend. [Note: Some of you will be reading this when your kids are already teenagers. It is never too late! It is just easier the younger that they are. As I said earlier teenagers often seem to forget what they learned when they were younger, anyway.]

In this case, teaching at the earliest time means when toddlers first begin to interact with others. When I see my little boy yank a toy out of his little sister's hands I might want to say, "Honey, it's not okay for you to take something from someone." I'm not saying that he's bad. I'm not saying he's not nice. I'm not judging him. I'm just stating a fact: It's not okay.

When he gets a little older, say, ages four to six and we're reading a book or watching TV together and a character does something that smacks of disrespect, I might say, "Do you think that man was being nice?" After he answers I might add, "I don't think he was being nice [either]. That's called 'disrespect.' That's something we don't do in this family. We always try to show respect." At this point all I want to do is to plant this seed: Here's the difference between respect and disrespect, and our family comes down on the side of respect.

At around age six or seven when he can defer gratification for at least a couple of minutes I might say, "When you see someone on TV do something that doesn't show respect, come and get me so we can talk about it." Or, "When someone does something at school that doesn't show respect, tell me about it when I get home."

All this is preliminary seed-planting, letting him know what I expect. Most of my teaching will come when I see him either showing or not showing respect.

If I observe he has just shown respect in some way I want to point out how much I appreciate it and why. "Thanks for showing respect. It makes the world a really nice place to live in."

When he does not show respect, it is a signal to me that we have more teaching to do. In this case I want to ask myself a few questions:
   - "Does he understand what respect is?"
   - "Does he understand why respect is important?"
   - "Does he understand what I expect about showing respect?"

As an eight-year-old he just knocked over his six-year-old sister. Here is a hypothetical dialogue [As an illustration I am purposely picking a kid who is making it difficult for me]:
   "Eric, was that showing respect?"
   "I don't know."
   "Well, tell me what you think respect is."
   "I don't know."

"Okay, if you don't remember that explains the problem. Let's explore what respect is. What does respect mean to you?"

"I don't know."

"Okay, tell me how you like to be treated."

"I don't know."

"If you don't know, that means I could treat you in any way I could think up and it wouldn't matter to you, right?"

[Seeing it coming] "Well, maybe not any way."

"Oh, so maybe you do like some ways better than other ways."

"Well, I don't like to be yelled at or hit."

"Neither do I. Would you say that was respect?"

"I guess not."

"Well, what about if you yell or push your little sister? Would you say that was respect?"

"She took my ball!"

"That's not what I asked. But since you brought it up, would you say what she did was respectful?"

"No!"

"Okay, it wasn't! Now, would you say that what you did to her in return was respectful?"

"How come you're not talking to her then?"

"Because right now I'm talking to you. I didn't know she took your ball. After we talk I'll have a talk with her, but right now all we're talking about is whether you understand what respect means."

"I do."

"Tell me what you think it means."

"It means not hitting."

"It means that to me too. Anything else?"

"That's about it."

"What about if some big guy came along and pushed you down. Would that be respect?"

"No."

"What about when you push down your little sister?"

118

"I guess not. But she took my ball."

"Okay, do you think there might be a way to handle it where you would still show respect?"

"I don't know. I guess I could ask her for it nicely."

"That sounds respectful. And what if she still didn't give it back. How would you still show respect?"

"I could tell you."

"That's one approach. It sounds like you understand what respect means now. Okay, thanks for the talk. I love you."

Now, I don't kid myself. Just because we've had this conversation does not mean from then on he will show respect in every situation. But at least I know now that he knows what respect means. He may have had an attitude, he may not have given me a very eloquent definition, he may not have covered all bases, he may forget later, but he was able to contrast respect and disrespect in terms of how he would act, and that's what counts for now.

The next time the issue of respect comes up I want to be on it again. As important as respect is to me I never want there to be a time where if he is disrespectful I let it go by, although if he or I are in a low moods I may want to say, "We'll talk about this later."

At age twelve I might overhear him talking back to his mother.

"Eric, is that showing respect?"

"I don't know."

"You've told me before that you don't feel respected if somebody yells at you. What about if someone talks back to you?"

"I don't know."

"Would you like it if I talked back to you?"

"I don't care."

"Really? So you mean it's okay if I start talking back to you?"

"If that's what turns you on."

"I wouldn't do it because I don't think it's respectful. Ask your mother how it made her feel when you talked back to her."

"I don't want to."

"So you must think it's not so good, otherwise you would have no problem asking."

Silence.

"Look, kiddo, I'm not mad at you. I'm not upset. But I think you hurt your mother's feelings and, to me, when you hurt someone else's feelings, especially your own mother, that's not showing respect. It's no different than hurting someone with your fists. It still hurts. And hurting someone in any way is not respect. Being respectful is really important to me. So when you feel up to it, why don't you apologize to your mother for not being respectful, okay?"

Here, I'm educating him a little more about some of the finer points of respect. I can tell from his responses and tone that he's in a low mood, so I don't want to push any more at this time. But I also want to be sure he is clear what is included within the definition of respect, and that it's so important to me I'm not going to let him off the hook.

Now, suppose we had that conversation and he keeps talking back. Then I've got to start asking myself, "Let's see, he understands what respect is, at least that talking back is not respect. He understands—at least I think he does—how important it is to me. What could be going on here?"

This assumes we have a good relationship, that we have followed what preceded this chapter of this book. I want to assume it is not defiance. I want to give him the benefit of the doubt. So I become very curious. There must be something about respect that he doesn't understand or he wouldn't be doing what he is doing. I wonder if doesn't understand for himself what is so important about it. Maybe he doesn't see the importance of it as I do.

Suppose he's fifteen.

"Eric, I'm really puzzled. Usually you do what I ask. But we've talked before about how important respect is and how talking back isn't respect, and you're still doing it. What's going on?"

"She's so stupid sometimes."

"That's an excuse not to show her respect?"

Silence.

"Why do you think I care about this so much?"

"I don't have the foggiest idea, dad. Why don't you tell me. You always do."

"No, I don't think I want to right now. I can tell by your tone that you look upon this whole thing with disdain. I'm really puzzled by this. I don't understand, and I was hoping you could help me out here. But I'll tell you what, we never have to bring it up again if you just treat her—all of us—with respect. Okay?"

Then I want to step back and observe.

I might notice that he doesn't treat her with disrespect all the time. Under what circumstances does he not? I might discover what he said is true: he only doesn't treat her with disrespect if he thinks she says or does something stupid. Then he treats her like dirt, as if that somehow makes it okay to treat her with disrespect. At such times he either doesn't see the connection, or his own feelings override it. So when he's in reasonably good spirits— perhaps when we're doing something nice alone together (so long as it doesn't ruin the moment)—I want to help him understand what he doesn't appear to understand.

"Eric, I noticed that you were right. Pretty much the only time you don't treat your mother with respect is when you think she does something that you would call stupid."

"Yeah."

[Note: I could go in many directions with this one, but I'm choosing to deal with it at the level of respect.] "It looks to me like you think if she acts stupid that's a license for all the rules of respect to go out the window. Is that true?"

"Well, no, dad. Not really."

"Then I'd really like to understand."

"It's not that I think it's right. It's just that she makes me so frustrated. Then I forget."

[Note: There are lots of meaty issues here, such as Eric thinking that someone makes him feel a certain way, instead of it coming from his own thinking. If I could help him understand how he is the source of his own feelings through his own thinking he would be less frustrated by his mother's actions. But I want to file that one away for another day because, right now, the main issue is respect, and I don't want to lose the thread.]

"Oh, I think I understand! So you're saying you don't think it's right at those times, but you can't help yourself. You lose yourself in the moment."

"Yeah."

"Oh, okay, I can relate to that. Sometimes I lose myself in the moment too. Everyone does. The one problem is she's still feeling disrespected."

Silence.

"Got any ideas about that?"

"Not really, dad."

"Well, if someone got really upset with you because he thought that you did something stupid and he punched you out, would it be okay if they just lost themselves in the moment?"

"I never do anything stupid."

"Well, suppose someone else thinks you did, even if you don't think so. Would it be okay?"

"No."

"What would you want from them instead?"

122

"Well, they'd have to do more than just apologize later. I don't want them to hit me in the first place."

"What would you want them to do?

"To tell me about it, tell me what I supposedly did wrong.

"How would you want them to tell you?"

"Nicely."

"So even though they've gotten lost in their emotions, you still want them to do that?"

"Yeah, they could wait until they calmed down."

"Do you think the same could hold true for your mother."

Silence. "I guess so."

"Okay, all I want you to do is watch yourself when you get that way. Just see yourself. Become aware of it, okay?"

"Okay, I'll try."

"And if you find it too hard, come and talk to me and maybe we can come up with some ideas about some other ways to look at this. Okay, kiddo?"

By seeing it in himself, instead of my coming down on him, I'm trying to get his own common sense to kick in. When it does—when he truly understands its importance— I know he will naturally show respect. I have to keep helping him see its importance—until he does.

REVERSING THE LOGIC

Midway through her sophomore in high school Jaime's grades suddenly plummeted. She had been hanging out at a park with a bunch of kids who at best lacked direction and at worst were taking drugs and being a bad influence. Yet, luckily, she began to gravitate toward a new group of friends who were very highly motivated and were excellent students. We were very thankful about her new choice of friends, but Jaime had not yet taken on their work ethic. She wanted simply to hang around them. Her report card averaged 67 for the term, and she was a very bright kid. Her mother confronted her.

In response Jaime became sarcastic and snapped, "I know I'm disappointing you. I know that I'm a big disappointment in your life because I'm failing. You think I'm a failure. You just think I'm a failure because I'm not as good as you, and I'm not you. Well, I'm who I am, and I'm not David, and I'm not you. Well, fine, I'm a failure!"

Judy looked at her. She knew, really Jaime was disappointed in herself. She knew Jaime didn't want to bring home a report card she herself wasn't proud of. Judy knew Jaime was capable of a lot more than that, dyslexia or not.

Judy then came out with one of the all-time great lines: "No, honey, you're not a big disappointment in my life. I don't feel like you're a failure. As a matter of fact I think that if this is what you want for your life—if you don't want to go to college, or if you want to go to a second-rate school, or not go to the school of your choice, whatever it is that you want to do—I think you're succeeding at it admirably. Because you're doing all the things that will keep you from going anywhere in your life. No, I don't think you're a failure. I think you're an enormous success. I think you're doing a wonderful job because you're going to get exactly what you've got your sites on."

For the first time in her life Jaime didn't answer back. She was speechless. Judy had stopped her dead in her tracks. She had turned the tables on her.

Judy knew Jaime had all kinds of dreams about going to a good, progressive college. Jaime was suddenly hit with the realization that if she kept on this track she would not get there. From that moment on Jaime did a complete turnaround in school. Despite how smart she was her dyslexia had kept her in standard classes surrounded by unmotivated students. At the beginning of her junior year she petitioned the school to let her into accelerated classes (where all her new friends were). No one in the school except her guidance counselor supported her. They didn't think she could make the grade. But Jaime knew she could and, to her credit, she persisted. She finally prevailed. In her senior year, in accelerated classes, she earned high honors.

Judy had turned her around not by telling Jaime what she wasn't doing right, force butting against force, but by joining with Jaime's force and, as in the martial art of Aikido, depositing it elsewhere.

I never would have come up with a line like that in a million years, but the great teacher/schoolmaster Marva Collins did. To reach her unmotivated or problem students she had been known to say [paraphrased], "I see your image. Is this what you'd really like to be in ten years? If not, what are you doing now to be where you want in ten years? Whatever you decide to be is your choice. You don't have to be here. In the streets nothing is demanded of you. Pick the box you'd like to live in, pick the corner you'd like to hang on. And that's a blessing. A lot of people don't know what they want to do."

It's tough to fight logic like that! It's hard to escape from that kind of logic. When people truly see what they're doing to themselves, there's no escape. When people are able to see the thinking driving them to nowhere or to destruction, there's nowhere to run and nowhere to hide from oneself. Such insights are when learning takes hold most.

OUR CHILDREN GROW UP
AND HIT THE ROAD

The day my son graduated from high school I suddenly wondered whether I had prepared him well enough for life. In a few days he would leave for the summer and then for college. He would be on his own. How would he do out there in the world? Did I prepare him well enough? Would he be okay without us?

It was a sad day. I wasn't ready for him to go. I loved him very much (still do!).

It was also a happy day—a day of gratitude.

Given the world we live in today and given the little I knew as a parent at the time, I thank my lucky stars every day that he came out of high school not abusing alcohol or other drugs much beyond experimentation, not getting anyone pregnant or contracting H.I.V., not being violent or a delinquent, not being depressed or suicidal, not being too unmanageable for his parents to handle. On top of that, he did well in school. He worked hard. He excelled at basketball. He had many friends, male and female. I thank my lucky stars.

But was he happy? I sometimes wondered. I thought he was, but he was also rather moody, especially when he woke up in the morning. But he was a teenager. And he had much to overcome.

When he was in the fourth grade Dave suffered a cerebral hemorrhage and nearly died. He had been in the kitchen cooking eggs, turned around to yell at his sister for something and out of nowhere he grabbed his head with the most intense headache imaginable. We thought he had the flu. Judy went to work and I stayed home with him. He became lethargic. Something didn't seem right. At some point it occurred to me to take him to the health clinic. Thank God for a very alert physician's assistant, Tonya. Something didn't seem right to her, so she sent him to the hospital for tests. Judy joined me there. Thank God for a very alert doctor who initially thought he might have meningitis. But it turned out a blood vessel in his brain had blown a gasket and he was bleeding internally. He was rushed in an ambulance to the Dartmouth-Hitchcock Hospital. Judy rode with him and I followed in the car. It looked bleak. The odds of survival were not good.

Somewhere in the middle of it Dave had asked me, "Am I going to die?" The words pierced my heart. I can still hear them ring in my ears today, and it still gets to me. I assured him he would not die (thank God I was right), but I've never been so scared in my life.

The doctors managed to stop the bleeding. Thank God again! He was out of immediate danger. But they had to wait a month or two before they could perform the surgery. The swelling in his head had to go down and the blood had to drain. But he was able to go back to school in between. Yet, there was some danger it could happen again before the surgery repaired the artereo-venus malformation condition that caused it, which unbeknownst to us he had been born with. As I understand it, instead of the blood transitioning gently through capillaries only a thin membrane separates the artery from the vein, which sets up a high-pressure situation that at some point can explode. That's what had happened. It was the same condition behind the deaths of a number of seemingly healthy twenty-or-so-year-olds who suddenly drop dead out of nowhere. Dave was lucky to have had it happen when he was so young. Children often have amazing recuperative powers. I volunteered to go to school with him for that month or so and sit in his fourth grade class to be on the spot in case any problem reoccurred. I learned a lot.

On top of that, poor Jaime suffered, as most of our attention was directed to David.

To make matters worse, after his major brain surgery we learned his learning capacity had diminished. The malformation and surgery had occurred in his left temporal lobe, a major learning center of the brain. Suddenly, he could no longer read well. He could no longer spell. He couldn't find words for things he knew. This frustrated him immeasurably. He plummeted from among the top of his class. It was heartbreaking to watch.

But he never wanted to be different. For a year he played basketball with a boxing helmet that I found for him in case he got elbowed in the head. Even though a boxing helmet is the coolest thing I could have found it was humiliating for him, but he was not about to give up sports, in which he excelled—thank God!. He refused Special Education. He worked so hard to regain his learning ability. Judy sat with him and helped him. And it worked. He did! On his own! It was hard! No one can know what he went through. I am so proud of him.

Yet we also learned he had bleeding into the frontal lobe of his brain, which is where behavior is controlled. We were told that, especially during his teenage years when all those hormones were kicking around, from time to time that scar tissue would get irritated, and when it did, once it reached a certain level he wouldn't be able to control his behavior. They were right!

He peaked in obnoxiousness at age fifteen. He was difficult for us to handle. Thank God for what we learned from Dr. Steve Glenn and his parenting course, *Developing Capable People*. We became fairly practiced at catching problem situations as soon as they were beginning to escalate—because once his scar tissue became irritated and it escalated beyond a certain point there was no stopping him.

It was still hard. Home was where he felt safest; therefore home was where he let off most steam. During much of that year I can't say we had a very good relationship with him. Things were strained much of the time. Poor Jaime suffered from that, too.

Toward the end of that year, serendipitously, I heard that tape by Darlene and Charles Stewart that I cited in Chapter 1. When Darlene said that no matter what horrible, crazy things her teenager did, she would stop trying to control him and just love him, "even if that meant bringing him cookies in jail," it changed my approach. I backed off and just tried to have a good time with him. Other than that, he was already a senior when I learned most of what is in this book so he never got the real benefit.

While our relationship with our children is what matters most I found myself wondering if my son had learned enough from me, whether he was prepared now that he was going off to college. So I asked myself at the time, "What do I want him to have learned as I send him on his way, off on his own? What do I want him to understand about life? What will help guide him through any difficult times?" I remember having the thought, "If I could only just tell him." Then I realized, "Hey, wait! I can!"

Here is what I came up with at the time that I wanted him to know, what I considered to be some words of wisdom from his Pops that would guide him reasonably happily through life, which I had just been learning. This is what I wrote down:

"Always know that—

• No matter what happens to you in life—no matter what ups and downs life may bring—you have all the health and well-being inside you that you will ever need, for it can never be destroyed, and it contains the wisdom to guide you through life.

• All you need to do to hear it is to quiet your mind or clear your head (which you can do in any way that suits you), and it will speak to you in the form of common sense thoughts popping into your head—so all you need to do is trust that it's there.

• When you feel frustrated or angry or irritable or down or bored or lazy or any of those emotions, the more you know that those feelings are coming from your own thoughts, and those thoughts are coming only from the way you're seeing things at the moment—and that can change—the less you will be controlled by those emotions.

The more you notice and are aware of what you're feeling at those times and the less you take those thoughts too seriously, because those thoughts are just tricking you by giving you faulty messages. The more you can't let go of something the further away you are from that health, but you're the one inadvertently making it up with your own thinking, and thinking changes.

- The more you understand that everyone sees the world in a completely different way from everyone else, and their world makes as much sense to them as yours does to you, and you can't talk anyone out of their world any more than they can talk you out of yours, the less you will be bothered and troubled by others.

- The more you recognize that you think differently about the same situation depending on your moods, and the more you wait until your mood rises before acting or saying anything, the better off you'll be and the better people will respond to you.

- If someone does you wrong or treats you badly [including a basketball coach] it's just that he's lost; his world is telling him to act that way and he is just doing the best he knows how to do at the time given how he sees things. If you can see him as innocent because he can't see a better way at that time and if you see him with compassion because he must be hurting to be taking it out on you, and if you don't take what he does or says personally you will be protected emotionally from whatever he does. (This does not mean not taking appropriate action when necessary.)

- The way you treat others creates what you get back in return.

- The people who achieve what they want in life believe they can do it, trust that what they want will fall into place for them, if they work hard to get it and don't give up.

- We will always be there for you if you need us.

- We will always love you no matter what you do!"

Dave became a rock and roll semi-star, playing bass with the very innovative African Rock blend band, Toubab Krewe. I'd say he ended up doing pretty darn well. I am really proud of him.

IX. SETTING LIMITS, AND DISCIPLINE

Up to now this may seem like a pretty laissez-faire approach to parenting. Not so! Kids need limits! They may not like the limits at the time but in the long run they appreciate them.

Discipline is the last chapter of this book for an important reason. Without the lessons of all previous chapters, disciplining children can cause detrimental results. So if you've picked up this book and just flipped ahead to this chapter, you're missing everything that will set the stage to make discipline work in the first place. By applying what is in the rest of this book I wouldn't be surprised if the need for resorting to discipline is cut by 90%.

I can hear some people say, "This is ridiculous! All we need to do is get tough with the kid."

Is this really true?

One day I watched a woman on a beach really get tough with her six or seven year old. She wouldn't let her get away with anything. I could hear her voice screeching even over the crashing waves. The mother would berate her kid, criticize everything she did. I could tell the woman herself was miserable and she was taking it out on her child. The poor kid got sand on the blanket and she was yelled at. She spilled something and the really tough mother was all over her case. She didn't put the sunblock on properly; the mother yanked the kid's ice cream away from her.

As soon as that mother turned her back the little kid stuck her tongue out at her. She did it every time the woman turned away from her. The kid was learning nothing except resentment. Poor thing.

Sometimes parents think they're making a difference, and they are—only not the kind of difference they think they're making.

Let's put discipline in context.

THE MEANING OF DISCIPLINE

Most parents think of discipline as either punishment or consequences.

Most of us have lost sight of what the word "discipline" means. It comes from the Latin word, "disciplina," which means "instruction" or "knowledge." The purpose of discipline is not to punish. Its purpose is for children to learn.

This means that everything in the previous chapter about teaching is really what discipline is about. Nearly always it is wise for teaching to be attempted before resorting to use of any consequences.

We could be the toughest parents on earth and thrust all manner of punishment upon our kids. If we are more powerful than they are, we can squelch the behavior, but is it working? If we have to repeat the punishment or consequences over and over again, no matter how tough we think our discipline is, the kid isn't learning. The discipline isn't working.

If we're going to discipline kids I would think we would want it to work.

BEFORE DISCIPLINE

The preliminaries to teaching, then, are also the preliminaries of discipline. To repeat them once again in this context. Before disciplining we would first be wise to-

- **access our wisdom from a clear or calm mind**

When we do not have access to our wisdom and common sense it is not time to discipline. When angry and upset we do not want to discipline. We want to be in a calm frame of mind. Sometimes our children will mis-behave in ways that make us want to bring down our wrath upon them. At those times we are just dying to punish right then and there. Barring an emergency, though, before attempting to discipline it is always best to first get over our anger or bother. So long as we're bothered by what our children are doing we will not act with the perspective we need. When upset we may do something we'll regret because we're not thinking right. Plus, whatever we say won't be heard as well. Instead, we want to step back, observe, listen and reflect, and look for the best answer before disciplining.

- **see the insecurity behind the troublesome or troubling behavior**

Let's say a kid goes to school stoned, is extremely disruptive, threatens his teachers, pushes drugs, brings a gun to school and bullies other kids. His behaviors are the least of the problem. Sure, they're big problems, but there is a much larger one. Imagine how troubled and lost and fearful and insecure this teenager must be to do such outrageous things to get by in life. In disciplining, then, the "troubledness" becomes the focus. This does not mean we shouldn't take responsibility to protect others or to uphold laws and rules; we absolutely should! The kid must be held accountable and cannot be let off the hook. *However, if we want this kid to change* it is most helpful for us to see the troubledness and what lies behind it. This in itself will cause our discipline to be conducted with compassion, which may allow an opening to get through. Otherwise, even though we can punish or even put the kid away for the rest of his life we stand little chance of changing his behaviors and, after all, isn't that the point?

- **insist on finding rapport, and be in a secure, responsive state**

Discipline has more power when conducted in an atmosphere of closeness and calmness. *Nothing is more powerful than taking a firm, unmoving stand without being upset.* Nothing is more powerful than being firm, calm and reasonable at the same time. If our kids think we are unfair, or if they hate us at the time, or if they see that our anger or upset is driving our actions, they then have an excuse to blame whatever is happening on something outside themselves. If they can blame what is happening to them on how mean we are they won't have to take any self-responsibility. Within an atmosphere of closeness, calmness and firmness nothing is left to blame (although they'll probably try to find something at first); they are forced to look only at themselves. As has been suggested repeatedly in this book, when kids sense negativity coming from us they automatically kick into "damage control" to protect themselves. This is why some kids try to get away as fast as possible, others talk back, some tune out, others storm out of the room or whatever they do. All are for the purpose of protecting themselves. Just as our children are experts at tuning in to our emotions it would help us to become experts at knowing immediately when something is not right with our feeling, our compass, our guide. It tells us whether we can discipline effectively in that moment or whether it would be wise to wait.

WHAT WOULD WE LIKE OUR
DISCIPLINE TO ACCOMPLISH?

As parents we would be wise to ask ourselves a very important question: Do we want our children to do what is right because they fear getting punished, or to do what is right because they are internally motivated to do what's right?

The choice is ours.

Every time we experience a problem with our children's behavior we are at a fork in the road. We can walk down one of two paths:
1. the moving-toward-well-being path
2. the moving-away-from-pain path

Through which path would we rather have our children motivated?

Children who grow up in an environment where parents mostly react to their "bad" behaviors tend to behave out of fear or to avoid pain. Such children tend to become either compliant or resistant. They find little motivation from within. They learn to react to things outside themselves.

Children who grow up in a secure environment where parents generally help them to look at a situation and learn from it tend to seek their own sense of well-being and happiness. This brings out their natural healthy tendencies. These children tend to be internally motivated to do what's right out of their own wisdom and common sense for their own well-being.

Simply being aware of this helps gauge our direction.

Some parents will say, "If my parents told me to do something and I didn't do it I'd get a beating and you can bet I did it then! What worked for me should be good enough for them!"

Again, we have to ask ourselves whether we want our kids to behave because they are running scared or because they see it is in their own long-term best interests to behave well.

It's true. So long as we are bigger than our kids, by sheer force we can get them to do what we want. Unfortunately this approach contains a few flaws. First, we can only to get them to do something by force when we're around them, and we are not around twenty-four hours a day. If kids learn to behave because someone is forcing them, when no force or controls are present many feel free to misbehave for there is no reason not to. Second, we may not always be bigger than they are. Third, as we've said before, they will be learning that when someone is bigger than you he can make you do whatever he wants, so if they find someone smaller they will likely return the favor.

Fourth, they won't be learning why certain things are right and wrong to be able to apply that learning to similar situations. So while brute force appears on the surface to work, it really doesn't.

If force won't work to the extent we may like, what will?

TAKING CHARGE

In her senior year of high school our daughter Jaime contracted mononucleosis. She had been on the run, burning the candle at both ends and it all caught up with her. She was barely able to move for about a week, then she was too sick to attend school for two weeks after that—a lot of school lost.

As kids are wont to do (not to mention many adults), as soon as she started feeling somewhat better she wanted to be out running around again. Judy and I saw it coming. In this situation we knew more than Jaime did. We knew mono stays in the system for quite some time and during the recovery period if a teenager overdoes it she can relapse badly. We told this to Jaime; it didn't move her. It was far more important to her to go to a party with her friends that night. She started to argue with us. All her friends were outside encouraging her to come.

Judy told her, "No! I'm not letting you do this!"

Jaime came running to me. "It's not fair!"

I said, "No, mom is absolutely right. This is where we're drawing the line."

Jaime became enraged.

We said, "Sorry, honey, this is what we think we have to do for your health."

Begrudgingly and angrily she stayed home.

When issues are really important to parents, parents simply have to draw the line. Young kids don't understand danger. Teenagers will place having a good time in the present above anything else. We certainly don't want to kill their enthusiasm for having a good time in the moment—we could usually use a lot more of that in our own lives—but we have to draw the line at what we consider really important. Not putting Jaime in a position where she might relapse was more important to us than anything else at the time.

As Dr. Steve Glenn said, we want to draw the line with firmness (if we say it, we mean it), dignity (not doing it in a way that will embarrass them or put them down) and respect (say it with kindness and caring). Where possible it is best to involve children in determining what is appropriate and inappropriate.

Sometimes it isn't possible. Sometimes parents simply need to step in and take charge, but that must feel right in the moment. It must come from a clear head, as opposed to a feeling of desperation. There is a huge difference.

One night as I was walking up the street I heard yelling and screaming coming from inside our house. It sounded terrible. I ran in to find David, who was seventeen at the time, practically beating on Jaime, who was fifteen. It apparently had something ridiculous to do with wanting to watch different programs on TV. David, who was larger than all of us, controlled the situation, refusing to watch anything but what he wanted to watch, refusing to move to his bedroom to watch his own TV, refusing to let my daughter into his room to watch his TV because she always messed up his room. In short, exacerbated by his frontal lobe irritation, he was in a mighty low mood.

So was his mother who was threatening to rip our son's cable box right out of the TV. One more time I was the one with the fresh perspective. [Note: Judy will have to be the one to write about all the times she bailed me out when I was caught up. For some strange reason I can't remember those as well.] By this time you know why I had perspective: I was not the one in the middle of it. Instinctively I knew I needed to take charge. For some reason I felt clarity. I quickly assessed the situation to see whether calm-enough heads could prevail for what I was going to say to be heard, despite high emotions.

I said to David, "Look, this can't happen here! You know this. [We had talked about it many times in the past but hadn't had the need for at least six months]. I don't think taking away the cable box is going to solve the problem. From now on, here's what's going to happen: If you can't agree on what program to watch down here in the den, then you've got two choices: 1) Either you let her watch what she wants down here and you go up to your room to watch, or 2) you let her up in your room to watch. You're the one with the extra TV. Does that make sense?"

No one could find any reason it didn't make sense. Even my son saw the common sense logic to it, even though he didn't like it.

"Okay, so we agree?"

I made sure that each said they agreed. If anyone tried to bring up something extraneous to the agreement I cut them off.

"We're just talking about this right now. That's irrelevant to this discussion."

I got an agreement.

"Secondly, Dave, you know you can't beat on her. You're much bigger than she is, and she could get hurt. I know you don't intentionally try to hurt her, but when you start doing that and people start getting wild, people can get hurt unintentionally—sometimes very badly! And I'm not going to risk it! It just doesn't make sense to put people in that kind of danger, does it? I mean, think about it. What if something really terrible happened and you didn't mean it?"

My intent was to get him to tap into his common sense—for himself. I didn't want him not to do it because I said so, or to do it for Judy, or even for Jaime's safety. I wanted him to see for himself, deep down inside, "it really isn't a good idea for me to potentially cause damage to somebody, especially to someone I love, even though I hate her sometimes." I wanted him to see the logic for himself. I saw something click within him, so nothing more needed to be said at that moment.

If he hadn't seen the logic and started arguing with me or started making excuses or was too overwrought to deal sensibly at that time I would have said, "We'll talk about this later." Then when emotions had cooled I'd try any way I could think of to get it to connect within him. I may find that he's too close to the situation to hear it, so I may have to draw inferences to a friend, or to myself when I was young, or to someone else with a different but similar problem. Sometimes it is best to teach impersonally so no perceived threat can impede learning. Ultimately I am committed to help him see it in whatever way I can.

If I had simply punished him I would be sending my son down the avoid-pain-and-fear path. He would be careful around his little sister—when he saw me coming. Or, I could try to help him see what is in his own long-term best interests. I wanted the latter path. I wanted to educate him about his choices for his own long-term happiness and satisfaction.

We want kids to do things because they understand, not because of a reaction to control. *If we know everyone has the wisdom to do what is in their best interests, wouldn't we want to help them tap into this wisdom and common sense? This is the key.*

So long as we back off enough to allow our emotions to die down, to relax, to clear our heads and regain our bearings, a wiser thing to do will occur to us. So we want to step back and observe and keep our mouths shut. This disengages us from our emotions and engages our wisdom and common sense, which then guides us to do what is best.

In the above example with my kids and the TV it may appear that I violated this point. Not so! For some reason I felt very calm and clear so I knew I had presence of mind enough to act. It felt right. That doesn't often happen to me. More often I need time.

As Roger Mills said, *the point of discipline is to help children regain their perspective so they can engage their own common sense.*

DRAWING THE LINE

Suppose a sixteen year old wants to borrow the car. The last time he borrowed it he left it with a thimbleful of gas.

What do we want to accomplish here? If I let him borrow the car now he will learn nothing. If I prohibit it without giving a reason he will learn nothing.

So I might say something like, "No, kiddo. I'm not willing to let you borrow the car when you leave it without gas. When you do that I risk getting stuck. That doesn't make any sense to me. Sorry."

"Gee dad, I'm sorry. I won't do it again."

"I appreciate that, I really do. But when you started to borrow the car I told you that you needed to be sure to bring it home with enough gas, and you said, 'Okay.'"

"Dad, I forgot. I'm sorry. I'll never do it again! Look, I really need to get to my friend's house. He's waiting for me."

"I'd love to let you take the car but I'm not confident enough that you'll do what I ask. Maybe next time."

He may go off the wall but that's got nothing to do with me. My job is to let him know I mean business here. If we wants the car in the future he'll do what I expect. It's not punishment. It's not even stated as a consequence. It's just logic on my part, common sense.

In this situation I may or may not let him take the car, but if I do I will need an agreement of expectations beforehand and confidence that it will be carried out. I'm only trying to ensure that if he's going to have access to a lethal weapon to drive around in I must have complete confidence in what he's doing. My getting stuck without gas is the least of the problem. With such a dangerous weapon if he forgets other things he could kill himself or others. How will he show me with deeds—not words—that he is responsible enough to have a car in his hands?

Teenagers often love to speed, sometimes to drink and drive. Nothing could be more dangerous! I need confidence that he's not putting himself and others in danger. I need absolute faith and trust that if he has the car he will not engage in these activities. Until I have this confidence, case closed! I'm not willing to take the risk. In telling him this I want to be friendly and calm, but firm.

What does speeding or alcohol and drugs have to do with gas in the car? It doesn't! But it has everything to do with being responsible, especially when one is riding in a dangerous missile. My confidence in his responsibility begins with having enough gas in the car. Through the gas issue that has presented itself, he has to learn how important responsibility is. He told me he would bring it back with enough gas. He didn't. If I can't trust him about gasoline, how can I be sure I trust him about anything involving the car? So he can't use it until he gives me reason to trust. There is no need to be angry. It is merely a statement of fact.

The same holds true for staying out late at night. I have to have trust that he is okay. I have to have trust that my daughter is okay. I don't want to be staying up late worrying about whether they're safe. If they want to go out they need to respect that I need confidence they will be safe and can trust them in that situation.

"I'll be okay, dad. There's no need to worry," won't wash. I need to be shown with deeds. If I don't see it in action, as young teenagers they can't go out. As older teenagers they can make their own decisions, but I still need to be able to trust. I'll even give them the benefit of the doubt, but how will they show me I can have confidence in them? It's really up to them. If they know what I expect, if it's clear, then they can decide what to do within those parameters. We may have to have some long talks until I am sure they understand and respect it. If they betray that trust I'm not willing to take the risk, period. Not for the sake of punishment, not for consequences, not to be mean, but because it's common sense.

In most parenting courses the emphasis is placed on the consequence. Here the emphasis is on the logic. I want my kid to see the common sense logic of it as I do, or to show me something else that makes even more sense to me that I haven't yet thought of.

Somewhere within every issue that arises a wise solution exists. We parents need only to step back and find it, then help our kids find it for themselves. If our discipline does not feel like common sense logic we would be wise to question what we're trying to accomplish.

RULES AND PUNISHMENT?

What if a child does something dreadfully wrong, is it not appropriate to punish?

The dictionary defines "punishment" as "subjecting someone to penalty for a crime, fault, or misbehavior."

If someone commits a crime (and gets caught) they have to pay a penalty. That's logic. It makes sense. The laws of the land define unacceptable behavior. Whether anyone likes the laws or not, when people know the general punishments for violations they make their own decisions about obeying those laws. Few people are surprised if they break a law and when caught have a punishment laid on them. That is common sense.

Families don't have laws. Many families have rules. Do rules fall in the same category as laws?

If everyone operated out of his or her own higher wisdom, so to speak, rules would be unnecessary. Family members would automatically respect each other, not put themselves or others in danger and generally do what is right and expected. If I had my way I would want my family to operate like that. Still growing up and learning, however, my children may not share my logic. They may not always be in touch with their common sense. Are rules then necessary?

Each family must decide this for themselves. The question is, who decides what the rules are and who decides what should happen if rules get broken?

Most families find when children participate in creating the household rules (if rules are deemed necessary) they take more personal responsibility for following them. To create rules together everyone in the family takes time to truly understand each other's logic behind their point of view and come to a meeting of the minds about what is best. If a rule is not working the parent would be ill-advised to change it on the spot. It is best to follow through with the rule then, but change it later through the same process that created it.

If rules are deemed necessary it is best if they are broad, general and few. Here are some examples of logical and reasonable rules:

- We will respect other people and their property.
- We will not put ourselves or others in danger.
- We will share responsibilities to keep the household running smoothly.

Rather than call these "rules" some parents choose to call them "expectations" or "understandings" or "agreements." "Here is what we expect from you." Or, "Here is what we've all agreed to." In any case, *everyone needs to understand what each of these really means so everyone in the household has a similar understanding.* Each needs to be discussed in detail. We can make up situations and talk about whether or not they violate the rules.

Once we've all agreed, if one child then hits another, we could say, "We all agreed to a rule here that we will respect each other. Is what you did respect?"

Does this mean we have to punish, to give penalty? Why would it be necessary? All we really want is for our children to understand what respect is, and to stick with it over time until *respect* becomes part of them. This is the teaching part of "discipline."

Only if they defiantly violate a rule would we want to consider going the next step. The next step is to demonstrate what we will and won't tolerate. Only then might we consider *having what they want to do be dependent on right action.*

Whatever happens in response to a rule violation must be logical from the point of view of the child. If a child does not do her homework, common sense dictates she might get bad grades. Suppose we decide to withhold meals? Most of us would never do that because it is completely illogical! Suppose we decide to withhold TV or her "smartphone?" Is that logical? It only is *if* the child watches TV or has her eyes glued to screens when she needs to be doing her homework and that is the reason homework is not getting done. Then it's logical. We can help the child make this connection to her common sense.

Suppose the child doesn't care about grades. Should the parent step in? How much does the parent care about grades?

After deeply listening to where our child is coming from about what she thinks about the importance of grades and why, one approach might be, with a good feeling, to say something like, "I want you to do your best. It makes life so much more enjoyable when people put their whole heart and soul into whatever they're doing at the time. When people get into the habit of doing this, for the rest of their lives they tend to find enjoyment in whatever they're doing. When they get into the habit of taking responsibility for what they have to do, they are likely to take responsibility for the rest of their lives. More opportunities seem to open up to them. So for those reasons I want you to do well. I know you have it in you. I know you can do it. I have complete confidence in you. I'm willing to give you all the support and encouragement I can, but in the long run it's your life. You have to decide for yourself what's important to you and what you want."

An alternative approach would be to clearly state expectations, period: "I expect you to do your best. I expect you to do well. I know you can do it, and I will do everything I can to help you."

Although I, myself, would be inclined to use the former approach because it has more of a chance to connect with the child's own common sense logic, either is okay. Neither is punitive. Both are clear. Parents can use whichever they can get behind and whichever will work best with their own kids.

Still another approach is to punish. Suppose I don't let her go out and play with her friends until she gets better grades. As with all punishment the problem is she may resent it and rebel. On the other hand, there is something to be said about fulfilling obligations before going out. On the other hand, going out to have fun might be what the child needs to clear her head, so she can then come back to the work with fresh, renewed energy. Which do we want? Which will work best for this particular kid in this particular situation? This is where deep listening comes in—listening to the child's logic. Does it make sense? Does it hold water? The parents may learn something. Then parents need to decide where they come down on each issue, then help the child to see the common sense behind their own view.

If I have to resort to punishment to get my children to do something such as homework I am losing the battle. I shouldn't be in a battle to begin with. I want them to see how doing well is in their own long-term best interests for their own sakes.

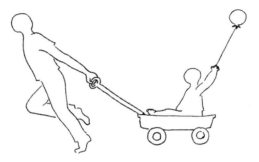

USING LIMITS AS AN OPPORTUNITY TO DISCIPLINE (TEACH)

Having children reckon with limits can help them learn how to handle their own emotional upsets.

Suppose a child does not want to go to bed. She gets upset. She becomes all riled up which leads to yelling, screaming and hitting.

Remember, first it would be wise for us to stay in our own health and not take it personally. Secondly, it would be wise to see the child's "lostness" so we can regain a warm feeling between us. The child has lost her bearings; we want to keep ours. Next, we want to help relieve her suffering. Then we want to help her see how, when she gets out of control, she is the one who suffers.

Getting upset happens to all of us and we all have to learn to get over it and calm down. We can learn to not get so upset in the first place. "We can help if you want by telling you what we do." [See Chapter IV–states of mind]

But here's the point: Being forced to reckon with the issue of "bedtime" makes this kind of discussion possible. Every situation is an opportunity to increase learning.

CONSEQUENCES?

If children won't go to bed a natural result occurs: The kids will be tired. They may not function well. They may be crabby and irritable. Over time they may weaken their immune systems and get sick. Not wanting to risk these, some parents learn to use "logical consequences." They ask, "What will make children go to bed if they won't go on their own?"

Instead, we could ask a more productive question. Reverse it! *"Why wouldn't a child want to go to bed?"* [We could ask this type of question whenever any issue arises.]

Suppose we had resorted to some logical consequence and later we learned the child resisted going to bed because she felt insecure. In such a case the use of consequences would only intensify her insecurity. Had we stepped back before relying on consequences we might have seen the child's insecurity. If we saw it, rather than apply consequences we would want to help minimize her insecurity.

Suppose, when we stepped back and listened we learned our child did not want to go to bed because he didn't need to; that he was not tired yet. Should we use consequences? What if, developmentally, he is outgrowing the bedtime we had set for him and the bedtime needs renegotiation? What if he were ready to stay up for another half hour or hour? We could say, "We're willing to try letting you go to bed later, but we'll see how you react in the morning. If you're too tired, or you're crabby (especially at us), then we'll have to go back to the way it is now. Fair?" The use of consequences would have clouded the issue.

Suppose we learned through observation that our child didn't want to go to bed because she wanted to be spending more quality time with us—suppose she needed more attention from us. Would consequences be in order? I think not. Maybe we only need to spend a little more time with her around bedtime, perhaps a half hour lying in bed reading or talking together. Relying on consequences may have killed this wonderful opportunity.

Suppose our child didn't want to go to bed because he wanted to watch a particular TV program that comes on past his bedtime. Every night? Are consequences in order? Why would they be? That's what DVRs or other recording devices are for. If the parent doesn't have a recording device, or if one "important" program is in question, is there harm in letting him watch it? After stepping back and weighing what feels right we can decide what is best. We can be flexible, so long as it does not compromise his ability to function or if he seems to get sick a lot. The use of consequences in this case would have inhibited this kind of healthy discussion and negotiation.

Suppose we observe that bedtime has become the battleground of wills; that our child uses bedtime as an act of defiance. Consequences must be in order here, right? Not necessarily! What would happen if we were to reverse the process, remove the battle?

George Pransky came up with a wild idea. He said something like, "Okay, we've been having trouble around bedtime, and what we've been doing has not been working. So from now on you can go to bed any time you want."

"You're kidding, right?"

"No. Really."

"What's the catch?"

"Nothing."

What George then did went something like this (although I'm remembering this from a long time ago and may not have it exactly right). The first night his daughters stayed up in front of the TV until around 2:00 a.m. before dropping off to sleep on the couch from exhaustion. The next day they could barely move, but they still had to fulfill their obligations and go to school. At school they could barely stay awake. They came home crabby. If they started to take a nap, he woke them up. "It's time to play now." The next night they tried to stay up late again, but they dropped off a little earlier. The next day it repeated but the third night they fell off to sleep even earlier. He overheard one daughter say to the other, "I think I'm going to sleep in my own bed tonight." Within a week they were going to bed on their own even earlier than their original bedtime had been.

I'm not sure I would have had the nerve to do that with my own kids, but it is impressive. More important, it worked. No consequences were applied, the desired result was achieved and his daughters learned an important lesson. If consequences were applied in this situation instead it may have given them something else to be defiant and willful about.

The real point is: *Often, we are too quick to use consequences and miss opportunities for real learning.*

If parents insist on using consequences they would be wise to ask themselves whether those consequences adhere to the values of rapport, respect and trust, or do they contribute to their kids running scared? Anything that adds an element of fear defeats the purpose. Anything that creates humiliation lowers kids' spirits. We want our children to function at their best.

We can spell out guidelines and responsibilities. We can ask if they understand. We can keep our eye on it until they do it. If not we can ask, "What happened here?" and make adjustments. Consequences may not even be necessary.

A STATE OF PUZZLEMENT

All kids want to do their best. If they don't seem to be doing their best some reason exists. Let's say a kid has a habit of rebelliousness. It is probably important to deal with the issue of rebellion. Suppose we're confused about what to do. How might we get to the heart of the issue? One way is to admit that we don't understand.

We could say, "I'm puzzled about why you feel the need to talk back to me. Apparently I'm not understanding something and I'd really like to. Tell me what I don't understand." If we get no response we might continue with, "Is it _____[and come up with some reason]___?" She'll usually tell me if I'm wrong. "Well, if it isn't that, what is it then? I really want to understand."

If we've talked about the issue of talking back and the child appears to comprehend why it's important not to talk back yet still seems to do it, this is puzzling.

We could say, "Kiddo, I'm puzzled by this. We've talked about not talking back and you say you won't, but you still do at times. Something doesn't make sense about this, does it? Is something wrong?"

Sincerely being in a state of puzzlement opens people up to new possibilities. It is part of deep listening. They themselves may not know why they behave as they do until we call their behavior into question. It can move them to a higher level of understanding.

DEFIANCE AND REACHING RESOLUTION

What if our kids aren't listening to us?

When a kid appears defiant or sees everything in a negative way and acts accordingly, what can we do?

First, don't forget, we use our incredible power of thought to see our children in any way we want. We could see them as defiant and self-centered and take what they do personally. We could watch the way our children act as if we were watching a movie and see what they're doing with interest and humor. We could see them with compassion because they're lost. *Given all the possible ways we could see our children, we have the power to see them in any way we want and we will experience the "real" feeling within our consciousness of whatever we think about them. Such power! We could feel humor or feel compassion or feel unpleasant feelings just by the way we see our kids.* So, first, even if they seem "defiant" to us, that may not be what is really going on.

Lying on a beach with warm sun upon us, usually we are completely relaxed. The reason we are so relaxed is because we have nothing on our minds. To see our kids as defiant and experience concern and worry about them removes us from our natural, relaxed state where wise ideas come to us. If they then do something that matches our belief that they are defiant—See! I told you he's defiant; this proves it!—we are coiled and ready to strike. We are off-balance. Instead, we could remain clearheaded and feel resolved to get to the bottom of whatever the behavior is that is appearing to be defiance.

Resolve means to make a firm decision. It means we think something is so important we're sticking with it. Resolve is persistence from a healthy frame of mind. We could feel resolve to deal with "defiant-appearing behavior" where the issue gets resolved to everyone's satisfaction in a healthy way. Or we could approach kids out of weakness (anger, irritation). With resolve we clearly see what is important to us and why, and hang in there until our kids see it.

Some people equate anger with resolve; that our kids see how much resolve we have by how much anger we show. But a close look reveals this isn't true. We can be angry and then let our kids off the hook. Conversely, we can feel calmness and clarity and be firm with total resolve, and it works better. When angry we act out of weakness. Out of weakness we tend to act with force, intimidation or coercion. Our kids feel threatened and react in turn. Would we not want to take action out of strength and a clear head (because it has a greater tendency to lead our children to understanding)?

Okay, back to our kid acting in what appears to be a defiant way. [Remember, if parents adhere to the approach suggested throughout this book rarely will they find their children defiant.]

It would be wise for us to ask, why would a child be defiant?

If we see children as defiant we become poised to do battle. When in conflict with children we are often brought down to their level. The opposite could occur; they could be brought up to our level (which assumes we're at a high enough level). Everyone is well-intentioned if we show love. If we stop fighting and drop our side of the ego game they have a far better chance of responding well.

"I'm puzzled. We agreed that everyone would participate in helping out with the household. We agreed the tasks would be shared. It is your turn to do the dishes and you look like you're having a hard time with it. I don't understand, and I'd like to."

I want to give him the benefit of the doubt. I'm not understanding something. I truly want to understand. This maintains rapport as much as possible, given that he doesn't want to do something, and it doesn't let him off the hook.

From asking questions and deeply listening suppose I hear my son does not see the logic of doing dishes. I try to explain my logic. It doesn't work. My kid doesn't see it as I do. I then have to decide whether I want to force the

155

issue. Is doing the dishes where I want to draw the line and make my stand? Gee, I don't know, there may be more important issues in life. But no, I'm not willing to let him off the hook—not because of something minor like the dishes, but because of its implications for all household responsibilities and for fulfilling agreements in general. I feel so strongly about that I have great resolve about this, but I also have resolve that it be worked out in a way that all parties will benefit, that learning will occur and it's done with a good feeling.

Is this a problem with all household chores or is it just dishes? Is this a problem about all agreements or is it just dishes? I have to ask myself and watch and listen carefully because either way dictates a different response.

Suppose I find he only seems defiant about dishes. Suppose he's perfectly willing to share all other household responsibilities and seems to keep all other agreements. One approach would be, "There are some things none of us likes to do but they still have to get done." Tough! That's the way it is. Well, it's true. But it's also true that some people find certain chores less objectionable than others and it might be possible to negotiate about "dishes" and still not let him off the hook about "objectionable household chores." Renegotiation doesn't let him off the hook, because I'm saying, "Okay, if it doesn't make sense to you, what does make sense that we can all agree on?" If we can find real agreement, then we stick with that. It is helpful for young people to learn the art of negotiation, and we can model it.

Maybe with some issues none of our logic holds water but it still feels important to us. Suppose I want my kids to be home for dinner so we can eat together as a family. I ask myself why it's important, and I can't come up with a good reason from the perspective of a child. All I can come up with is it makes me feel good to have the family together for dinner. "I just want this" is not real compelling logic; it's just a desire I have. In that case I could say, "Humor me on this one. I like being with my family. Would you be willing to do this for me as a favor?"

We have to be careful. We can't use "favors" for too many things that don't make sense to them. We need to decide what's really important to us and take our stand there.

But back to defiance. What if neither "dishes" nor "household chores" nor "agreements" is really the issue? What if the issue seems to be that my teenager appears to be developing an unhealthy, defiant attitude in general? What then?

Again, we go back to assessing: Is our own feeling right? Do we have rapport? (doubtful)

Have we deeply listened enough through puzzlement and sincerely trying to understand so we understand why he is acting defiant—what is behind it? Have we attempted to turn the issue into a nonthreatening learning experience?

Okay, but suppose we're still not getting anywhere? What do we do then?

Here it is helpful to introduce something else I learned originally from George Pransky.

CREDIBILITY

Dr. Pransky refers what he calls the "Credibility index." If we tell kids to do something and they don't do it, and nothing happens, the next time they will wait to see if we really mean it before they act. We will have less credibility. If we lose our credibility it can escalate to the point where they won't even hear what we say.

Taking a step back, what does it say to a child when we say something and don't mean it? What message does it give when we say we're not going to let a child do something and then we let her do it? What does it mean when we say that if she doesn't come now we're going to leave her behind, and then we don't? If we say something we've got to mean it, or we lose credibility.

It is unwise to tell children to do something if they are not going to end up doing it. Therefore, we need to be careful what we ask or demand of them. If we order it, it must be enforceable; otherwise it is best not to ask. Sometimes, inadvertently, we can ask our kids to do things that are inappropriate to their age, such as asking a three year old to remember to pick up his toys after a TV program is over. Sometimes we tell teenagers things out of anger that are unrealistic, such as, "You're grounded for the next ten years."

By the time our kids are ready to deal with some of the toughest issues, such as hanging out with the "wrong crowd," or drugs, we would be well-advised to have good credibility.

Credibility comes with having resolve about what we say. Credibility comes when we get behind something and mean it, and when we follow through. If a kid doesn't do something we've asked, we might first say something like, "You probably didn't remember this but I asked you not to talk back and you agreed." This allows the kid to regroup while keeping our credibility high, because we're not forgetting it.

Sometimes we can require something that in retrospect was a mistake, such as saying a kid cannot hang out with a certain group of friends. True, we may not like this group of friends. We may think they're a bad influence. But *what we really care about is his own behavior*. To say he can't hang out with a group is often unrealistic because at least at school, for example, he *will* hang out with those friends when we're not around to see it.

If we make a mistake requiring something like this we can admit it. "I'm sorry. I shouldn't have required that of you. It was unrealistic. But here's what troubles me about your hanging out with this group. I'm concerned that some of their behaviors that are against the law will rub off on you. I'm concerned you'll be in the wrong place at the wrong time if they get busted, and it will be guilt by association. It is far more difficult to resist if a whole group is doing something and you're not, especially if they're calling you a 'wuss' or whatever. But what I do care about are your own behaviors. I simply cannot accept certain behaviors. I care too much about what happens to you. How can we come to a meeting of the minds about this?" Here, our credibility has been restored. I'm not letting him off the hook about the important issue of his own behavior, but I'm willing to talk more about it and see what we can reasonably come up with.

Ultimately, kids need to have respect for "the writing on the wall." If we say it, we mean it. Otherwise, we lose credibility and it is far better not to have said it in the first place.

BREAKING THE PATTERN

Suppose we hear, "I'm doing it anyway; I don't care what you say." Whoa! That sounds suspiciously like defiance.

Or suppose we hear, "Okay," and then we find out they're ignoring us and doing it anyway. Whoa again! Could that be defiance too? Passive defiance!

First, I know I could punish. I could make him stay in his room for a week or a month if I wanted to. I'm the parent, goddamn it and what I say goes! I could take him behind the woodshed. I could do lots of things to punish, or I could use consequences. But for the health of our relationship and his learning I could also step back before I pounce.

I could ask myself what I have done in response to situations that have led up to this moment. Hmmm. What has he learned up to now that perhaps we didn't intend? Suppose we have treated our children in ways that, in retrospect, we now see were detrimental to our relationship or to his learning. Have our actions contributed in any way to his acting defiant? Suppose we decide to approach our kid differently. Here we need patience because our kid has built up expectations based on what happened in the past. He will continue to act the same way until he realizes it's a new ball game. A change may not happen overnight. It takes commitment and persistence.

If a pattern has built over time, if we want the kid to change, we may have to change. We can go to a child and say, "I can see I've been handling things in the wrong way and it has caused problems. I'm really sorry. I want it to change. I'm prepared to start with a completely clean slate. But to do so I'd like us to talk things out so we can end up with a meeting of the minds instead of a battle. What do you think?"

160

Because we're taking responsibility for our part and apologizing and starting fresh we can forgive everything that happened in the past. This clears the decks. Now, we are drawing the line anew, and we have resolve about it. The message is, "We're starting fresh now, but you do understand this cannot happen again, right? That's very clear, right? Is there anything you need from me that will help you not do this unacceptable thing, or can you do it on your own?" This might be a real shock to the kids system—he may never have been asked before, just landed on—but it may help to move things forward.

WHEN THINGS HAVE GOTTEN OUT OF HAND

A friend of ours, Harriet, a single mother with four children, was at her wits end. She knew her fifteen year old daughter, Emily, was drinking, smoking marijuana, in all probability taking L.S.D., having unprotected sex with her boyfriend (who had already been picked up by police for attempting to rob a store), being disruptive in school, failing subjects, often being truant and being generally incorrigible at home. Whenever her mother attempted to take control Emily would fight, sometimes with her fists. In short, the situation had gotten completely out of hand. Harriet expressed grave concern about the effect this must be having on her three younger children. She sought my advice.

I asked Harriet what she had done to try to intercede.

Harriet told me that she tried to set limits but Emily scoffed at her and didn't obey. For example, when Harriet wouldn't drive Emily to see her boyfriend Emily attempted to jump out of the car going 50 miles an hour until her mother relented.

Harriet said she showed Emily love. She told Emily that no matter what she did she would always love her but that her behavior was unacceptable and had to stop. Emily ignored her.

Harriet said that when she was in a low mood she tried not to talk with Emily but sometimes she couldn't help it when things got out of control. She had said to Emily, "We've got to talk this out. Things can't go on like this." Emily sassed her back.

Harriet tried to take Emily to counseling at "youth services," but after a couple of sessions Emily refused to go back because "they won't tell me what I should do."

Since Harriet asked for assistance, let's take a step back and ask ourselves what we know.

* First, the drinking, the drugging, the sex, the truancy, the disobedience, the incorrigibility, are only the secondary problems. They are merely symptoms of the larger problem of insecurity. For some reason Emily feels so insecure she thinks the only way she can have fun, or for that matter get by in life is to act in these ways. Emily is hurting badly and her actions are only manifestations of her pain. Harriet has done nothing to deal with Emily's insecurity; in fact, what she's done has increased it.

* Harriet may think she is showing her daughter love but her daughter is not feeling it. Fist fights at home are not exactly the embodiment of living in an environment of love. This relationship has no rapport. Instead of a meeting of the minds they have a butting of the heads.

* Clearly, Emily is not connected to her innate health, wisdom and common sense. She is too caught up to see it. When her mother tries to land on her Emily scrambles to protect herself. She loses herself.

* Unless something changes with Emily's thinking, the behaviors will never change. Only if Emily's thinking changes will the behaviors follow.

* Even though Harriet knows that when she is in a low mood she shouldn't try to control or talk with Emily, Harriet can't help herself (or at least thinks she can't), so she does.

* Harriet is not listening deeply enough to Emily to know what the real, underlying problem is. She does not understand Emily's world, how Emily sees it, so how could Harriet possibly know the best thing to do?

* Somewhere along the line Emily did not learn respect. She does not respect her mother. Emily does not believe her mother will follow through with her threats, so she has her over a barrel.

* Even though Harriet didn't mention this, I also knew something else. Harriet's house was in chaos, cluttered beyond recognition. She was a hoarder. It was not conducive to calm, sane living. Emily couldn't stand being there, yet she was not willing to help her mother make the house more sane. Emily didn't see the point or the benefit. Further, the house reflected the state of Harriet's mind.

If this is what we know, then how should Harriet proceed?

First, how much is Harriet willing to change? If Harriet truly wants a change in Emily how much is she willing to get all the points above back on track? If she isn't willing she cannot expect much change from Emily.

Further, Harriet is so overwhelmed about her own life that she needs help herself. If nothing in her own thinking changes she will continually feel overwhelmed. She will continue to feel that everything, including Emily, is out of control. Unfortunately, to her detriment Harriet is an expert at making things appear okay. She has been to traditional therapists and pulled the wool over their eyes. [Note: She hadn't seen a Three Principles Therapist, which is based on the same principles as this book.]

Harriet told me she was willing to get help for herself but she never followed through. My guess is she never intended to, probably because she was too embarrassed. Given that Harriet won't go out of her way to change, is there anything she can do for Emily?

While not ideal, Harriet could still change Emily's course by changing the way she deals with all points listed above. Nothing Harriet has tried so far has worked. She has zero credibility with Emily. Therefore, it is not wise to try anything again that Harriet has already tried. Harriet needs to reverse the process.

If Emily is acting out of insecurity the antidote is security. Emily needs to feel love and acceptance for who she is deep down inside. Harriet believes she is showing love, but she certainly isn't showing it in the moment so Emily feels it. Harriet needs to find that loving feeling in her own heart for her daughter. She needs to see beyond the presenting behavior to her spiritual essence, to the way Emily was as a beautiful little baby. She needs to see the lostness. When Harriet feels it herself, and when it feels like the right moment, when no one else is around, she needs to have a heart-to-heart talk with Emily. But Harriet's heart must be in the right place. Is she in a good state of mind? Does she feel love in the moment? Does she see Emily's innocence and her distress? When Harriet truly sees Emily's distress her heart will go out to her. In will rush a warm feeling. This is the time to talk.

Through an honest, respectful discussion Harriet and Emily need to come to a meeting of the minds. Harriet needs to listen very carefully to what makes Emily behave the way she does. But Emily won't tell her if asked directly. She may not know herself. What doesn't Emily understand? Why does she talk back to her mother? What is not right about that? Why should she do her homework? None of her friends do! Why shouldn't she have sex or take drugs? All her friends do and they don't look any worse off to her. Why should she take care of herself at all? Why not just commit suicide, then? What does she care about? Where can a meeting of the minds be found?

Suppose no meeting of the minds can be found. Suppose Emily doesn't respond. Suppose Harriet won't even have this kind of talk. Suppose she says, "We've already had talks and they don't work." Can she still be helped with Emily?

Something can still be done, although even less ideal. When things have gotten out of hand, sometimes teenagers and other kids may need to be brought up short to get their attention. Harriet needs to take charge. She needs resolve.

She could say something like, "Emily, honey, I love you so much! I care about you so much! In fact so much that I can't bear to see you damage your life. But I've tried everything I know how. I don't know anything else to do. I'm so sorry we've gotten into fights. That's not right. That's not the way I want to be with you. This is not the way I want to live. I just didn't know anything else. But I'm so sorry. I hope you can forgive me."

At this point Harriet would want to watch Emily's reaction very carefully. If there is any possible meeting of the minds at this point Harriet could grab it and listen very carefully, talk it out and see what conclusions they can reach together about how things can be different.

If no meeting of the minds can be found and nothing improves Emily needs to learn that her mother is serious about a new course of action, and she will follow through. Harriet, as a parent, could come to the conclusion that she is no longer willing to support Emily's behavior. The question then becomes, "What does she want that I have?"

Harriet needs to ask herself, "Okay, Emily is not obeying anything I ask. *What does she want from me?* Money? The use of the car? To be taken places when she wants to go?"

Harriet has to be willing to take a stand. With a loving feeling Harriet can continue with something like, "Emily, honey, I decided I am no longer willing to be treated the way you're treating me. This may not be right, but from now on if you want something from me you have to treat me with respect—and not just at the time you want something. All the time! I can no longer go on like this. All I know is I am no longer willing to put up with you treating me like dirt and having your brothers and sisters learn this behavior from you. So if you continue your behavior, if you want to go places you can find your own transportation. If you want money you can earn your own. You can do what you want, but don't expect me to provide you with what you want. Living together is a two-way street. My responsibility is to give you food, clothing, and shelter, but that's all I have to do. From now on that's all I will do. As soon as you demonstrate that you've changed I'll go back to providing those other things you want."

When parents start messing with what a kid really wants from them, it can work wonders.

But what if even then Emily still does not respond? Suppose she says she doesn't care whether her mother gives her anything or not, and her behavior remains as outrageous as ever or gets worse. Is there anything else Harriet can do? There is, but only if Harriet is willing to resort to truly drastic measures. If Harriet were only willing to change course earlier, what follows would not be necessary.

Emily may need to be startled out of her world. Right now Emily's world appears to be working in her favor. It protects her, or so she thinks. She's having fun. She's getting away with what she wants. Sure, she has fights with her mother from time to time, but it doesn't get in her way too much. Emily needs to be shocked out of it all.

Still with a loving, caring feeling Harriet could say something like, "So Emily, honey, I don't know what to do here. I don't know if this is right or not, but I've decided I cannot accept you doing these things if you're here under my care. So the next time you do something I consider damaging to you, me or this family I will call social services and tell them you are beyond my control and they need to put you in a shelter home for a while until we can reach some agreement on an acceptable way for us to live together and acceptable behavior. God knows I don't want to do this in the worst way, but I simply don't know what else to do."

If Emily's behavior doesn't change Harriet *must* follow through, no matter how painful it is. This cannot be an idle threat. Some people would call this, "Tough Love." Emily must understand that the door is always open. There is always another chance to work things out.

Hopefully such a drastic measure would never be necessary. Hopefully Emily would suddenly realize the line has finally been drawn in the sand. She will suddenly understand what will happen if she doesn't change; that her mother is finally serious and resolved. Why? Because her mother is using a completely different tone and a completely different approach. Emily may sit up and take notice and say to herself, "Oh wow, mom is really serious here!" This realization would give Emily an opportunity to get back on track without her mother having to implement the extreme. If Emily tries to call her bluff Harriet needs to get right on the phone and make that call.

Please remember this drastic measure is *only* suggested when things have gotten so far out of control that the parent truly does not see any other way. Some time in a temporary shelter may give both parties the time they need to step back enough to regain common sense and decide what they want for themselves. Later they can come together knowing what is on the line and what needs to happen. In most cases clearer heads will prevail. This also implies Harriet will have had to do some homework beforehand to learn what her options are if a child is without or beyond the control of her parents.

But before having to resort to this drastic action, don't forget, Harriet could decide she herself has to change. She could go out of her way to be sure all those points above are in place. If she is truly concerned about having a breakthrough with her daughter and having this situation not adversely affect the life of her family she must take a huge step back and ask herself, "What about the way this family lives and interacts with each other makes it difficult for Emily to be here reasonably?" The idea is not to analyze the answer but to put the question on the back burner of her mind and go about her business. An answer will surface when she least expects it, when her mind relaxes and clears. That's when she will hear wisdom speak. She needs to truly listen for an answer but her mind must be clear enough to hear it.

Through listening Harriet may see that Emily can't stand the chaos in that house, the mess, and she wants to escape it all. What is Harriet willing to change? What is she willing to do differently to make this home a more comforting, calm, loving, inviting place to be? Why wouldn't a child want to be in her own home?! Why would she want to be on the run all the time? There is always a reason. Emily is not the only one with the problem. It takes two to tango, two to create the difficulties. Is Harriet willing to get real help for herself?

Ultimately Harriet has at least three choices: 1) She can keep things as they are and stay tortured by Emily; 2) She can have Emily removed from the home; 3) She can show her daughter that she, herself, is willing to change. Of course Harriet can only change if her thinking changes. If she takes a step back, sees what she needs to do and finds she can't do it, she may need help. How important is it to get back to a good relationship with her daughter? Harriet can only answer that for herself.

To have privileges be dependent on responsibilities is not unreasonable so long as the two are linked by common sense. Yet to work best, even this must be conducted within the proper environment and after the rest of the learning process has been attempted. Having a child removed from the home is, obviously, a measure of absolute, last resort, to be used only when things are so out of control that no other choice appears possible. None of it would be necessary if Harriet would only go through each of the points made earlier and adjust accordingly.

AND IN THE END . . .

This book is based on the premise that in nearly every situation that arises parents will know what to do—if they listen closely to their hearts, to their wisdom.

To hear what is in our hearts, our heads need to be clear, to calm down. This happens when we step back from the situation at hand, disengage from our emotions (from our thinking), and allow the mind to quiet so we can hear and see new, hear wisdom speak. To enhance our potential for receiving insight we can set our intention for our minds to receive the answers we need by asking ourselves the right questions.

It is extremely helpful to understand, in our hearts, that both we and our children have an essence that contains automatic well-being, peace of mind and wisdom and common sense. To help our children most in life we want to help them know how to engage it. If we can help them calm down, they can access it more readily. If we create around them that loving, caring, supportive, respectful, lighthearted environment and breed rapport, they can access it more readily, for that is what is in their hearts just dying to come out.

The more we are aware of our feelings and moods in the moment and allow them to guide us about when we can trust and follow our thinking so we know the best time to take action or speak, the less we will get in the way of allowing their health to rise to the surface.

The more we see our children's troubling and troubled behavior as acting out of insecurity, which means our job becomes to help them feel more secure, the more we will engage what is in their hearts.

The more we listen deeply to what our children are really trying to tell us and understand how they see their worlds, the more we will know how to proceed with them, and the more they will want to listen to us.

Within that kind of atmosphere, the more we help them learn to engage their own wisdom and common sense about what they need to understand to get along well in the world, and the more we help them know with certainty what is expected and important to us and why and where we draw the line, the better off they will be, not only with us but in the entire rest of their lives. And the more we have resolve and patiently stick with it until it becomes part of them, the better off they and we will be.

In so doing we will be bring out the best in our children, and they will demonstrate it through their behavior.

In short, love your kids for who they *really* are and help it come forth. The rest is merely detail.

Now, read this book again, and have a great time with your kids!

AFTERWORD

Shortly before this book went to press (the first time) we received this e-mail from Jaime toward the end of her freshman year at college:

> I just want you and Mom to know that you mean the world to me. I miss you very much, but I appreciate all you let me do and what you have taught me. I chose you for a reason, and now more than ever I know why. Many people tell me how envious they are of my relationship with you, and I take it less for granted now than ever. I love you both more than words can tell. I miss you very much. Tell Dave I love him.

I guess we didn't do so badly, after all.

THE ESSENCE OF PARENTING FROM THE HEART

* Be sure children are living in an environment of love, caring, support, lightheartedness.

> The feeling we have in the moment when interacting with children *is* the environment the kids are living in.

* See children as the health, wisdom and common sense deep within that is ready to be actualized at any moment.

> When our minds are calm and clear we have access to wisdom and common sense.

*See children in their innocence, as thoughts they are unaware of that have made them innocently get off track and lose their way.

> See children as always doing the best they know how at the time given the way they are seeing things.

* See ourselves in our moods, and understand that in low moods our thinking is giving us faulty messages, and if we trust it or believe it and follow it at those times, we will not be effective.

> See children in their moods and understand when they say or do things out of an insecure, reactive state there is no need to take it personally because it is only their mood talking.

* See children's troubling behavior as acting out of insecurity (or out of a low mood or what we're saying doesn't make sense to them), therefore we want to help them feel more secure and help them find their way.

Watch children with interest, as opposed to being caught up in their craziness.

* Before teaching or disciplining be sure we step back, observe and listen deeply, so wisdom is available to guide.

* Before taking action ask, "What will my kid be learning if I say or do this?"

Instead of laying our conclusions on kids, help them understand what we took into consideration in reaching our conclusions.

* Ask, "What is most important to me about my children's behaviors?" and "Where do I need to draw the line?" Then with caring, patience and resolve help guide kids to that end.

c. 1997 Jack Pransky

APPENDIX I

In the first two editions of this book I included an appendix called "If You Insist" stating, "Despite what this book suggests about the fallacy of relying on parenting techniques, some parents still insist upon using them... [and]... will not be satisfied that what is offered in the main body of this book is enough." But no one I knew of who read this book ever needed to use it. So instead, this time I offer a completely different kind of Appendix: I present a couple of my favorite parenting examples from two of my other books: *Somebody Should Have Told Us!* and *Prevention from the Inside-Out.*. Both are beautiful illustrations of what *Parenting from the Heart* is talking about.

The following is an excerpt from *Somebody Should Have Told Us!*, Chapter X titled, "We're only as stuck as we think we are."

Alyson and her teenage son, Mark, were stuck.

They both showed up at a training I conducted on Maui. They knew I had written *Parenting from the Heart* and thought I might be able to help with an issue of great concern to both of them.

Mark had recently turned sixteen and got his driver's license. His parents gave him a car. They told him not to speed. He said he wouldn't. It took only a few months for Mark to be involved in five speeding incidents, one resulting in a blown tire on a lava-rock road.

This was unacceptable. Mark's father wanted to yank the car away from him forever. Alyson, the mother, thought this was too harsh; she wanted to put her foot down but was afraid of alienating Mark. Mark knew some kind of discipline was in order but feared what might happen. Both badly wanted a satisfactory resolution. Both were stuck. Both wanted me to address this incident. The other training participants agreed. They were curious about how I would handle a situation like this.

I had already talked with them about the three principles—Mind, Consciousness and Thought—and both Alyson and Mark had found it interesting. Our rapport felt right. So I questioned them and listened deeply. It was apparent they had an excellent relationship for a mother and teenage son.

Alyson said, as a consequence she was thinking of not allowing him to attend a summer musical play he was involved in. Mark desperately wanted to be part of this play.

I became puzzled. If the issue was the car and speeding, what did a summer play have to do with it? If I couldn't follow the logic I was pretty sure Mark couldn't. To me it only confused the matter.

I was also puzzled by Mark's behavior. I asked him if he knew what the expectations were for driving and having this car, and he said yes. Something didn't compute.

"This is curious," I said. "I'm wondering why someone who knows the expectations would violate those expectations?"

Mark said. "I don't mean to. There were just these situations..."

"So violating the expectations is okay, given certain situations?"

"Well, no, but..."

I let him ponder that a moment and turned to his mother. "Alyson, what is it that bothers you most about his behavior?"

She thought a moment. "Well, two things, really. First, if he's not going to be responsible, driving a car is really too dangerous. He could kill himself if he speeds."

I stopped her and turned to Mark. "Can you understand that from her perspective?"

He said, "Yes."

I turned back to Alyson. "What's the second thing?"

"This is the way it is all the time with Mark. I mean, I know he means well and he's a great kid, but often I have to tell him many, many times before he'll pick up anything that I ask him, or if he'll feed the dog, or things like that, and sometimes it doesn't even get done."

This interested me too. I said, "Well, if you have to tell him many times to do things it sounds to me that he doesn't think you're serious. So why should he think you're serious about the speeding? He doesn't have to comply as long as he doesn't think you're serious."

Alyson looked sheepish. The corners of Mark's mouth betrayed a tiny smile.

I turned to Mark. "Mark, you've told me you know what the expectations are, so what's on your mind when you speed?"

"I don't mean to. It's just that I forget."

Alyson chimed in. "Yes, he's so totally involved in whatever he's doing that he just forgets to do what he's asked—not just about the car but with many things, as I said."

"So the problem, then, really isn't the speeding. The real problem is 'forgets.' Speeding is a symptom of 'forgets.' But because speeding is such a dangerous symptom, you really need confidence that he's not going to speed, despite the fact that he forgets, right?"

"Absolutely."

I turned to Mark. "You can understand why a parent would need confidence that if you're going to be riding around in a lethal missile, she needs confidence that you're going to be safe, can't you?"

"Yes, I understand that."

179

"So, Alyson, this absolutely needs to be solved to your satisfaction because it's so dangerous. But in trying to solve it, if it doesn't get at the underlying issue of 'forgets' it's not going to work, see?"

"That's true, so what am I supposed to do? I know he's not doing it on purpose, but I can't be worrying that he's going to be in danger. What would you do?"

"What I would do isn't important."

"But I would really like to know what you would do."

I sighed. "Well, I would want my wisdom to speak to me. Knowing he's not doing it on purpose but knowing it's too dangerous to continue on like this, if it were me I would wipe the slate clean as of this moment and start fresh. But I would make it very clear that if he violates the speeding or car safety agreement even once more, good-bye car, period, no questions asked. If he knows that up front, then it's his decision what to do."

"Yes, that's great. That makes it real clear, and it's not too harsh because he's been given this new chance."

"But Alyson, if he did speed you'd absolutely have to follow through, you know? Otherwise this could go right back to the old pattern of thinking by letting him off the hook. Because you would feel bad about having to follow through and really take the car away from him, right?"

"I know."

Mark said, "That's fair."

I said, "Mark, if I were you I wouldn't be so quick to agree with this. I mean, there's a lot riding on it, literally, because if you violate this rule, no more car. I mean, what if you forget? We still haven't done anything about the issue of 'forgets.'

"No, I could do this."

"I'm not sure you'll be able to, honestly. I've noticed the speed limit is really low here on Maui. One little forgetful moment and it's all over, and you have a habit of forgetting. So I'm curious: What goes through your mind when you're asked to do something, before you forget?"

Mark reflected a moment. "I'm really involved in something, and I say to myself, 'Okay, just a minute until I finish up what I'm doing.'"

"And then?"

"I get involved again and don't think about it any more."

"Okay, so that's your habit. I can see how you're not doing this on purpose. But the fact is, what you're supposed to be doing isn't getting done. What about when you're driving?"

"Like I said, that's only when a special circumstance comes up, like if I'm running late or something."

Alyson chimed in. "He's late and leaves at the last minute because he gets so involved in what he's doing that he forgets to leave in time."

"Mark, so that's an excuse to speed?"

Mark said, "Well, I don't want to be late."

"So besides 'forgets,' the problem is also 'exceptions.'"

Sheepishly, he said, "Yes."

"Okay, remember what I said before about Thought creating our experience? In this case you're getting a double dose. Not only are you using your incredible gift of Thought to tell yourself, 'It's more important to finish what I'm into than do what I'm told right now,' and 'It's better to speed than to be late'—see, both of those thoughts give you a 'real' experience in your Consciousness that looks like it's truth—but on top of that, those thoughts *lead you* to behaviors that end up getting you in trouble."

Mark said, "Oh, that's what you meant before when you said it's an illusion."

"Yes, your thinking is tricking you, and you're falling for it, and it's leading you to the point where you're about to lose your car. And it's all started by believing those thoughts that pop into your head. But you don't have to! That's your protection. Because if you don't believe, 'I can just put off what I have to do for a moment' or 'I'm late so I'd better go faster'—if you allow thoughts like that to come in but then pass right on out—they can't do you any harm. And what will be left is listening to your own wisdom, which is telling you the best thing to do. That's your gut feeling telling you what's right. So you're going to have to be careful about believing that thinking, because it will end up with you losing your car. You see that?"

"I do. I won't speed if I don't pay attention to what those thoughts are telling me."

"Right! But right now you've got a habit of that kind of thinking, so you're definitely going to have those thoughts. That's what you'll want to keep an eye on: the thinking that, for example, is behind putting your foot down on the accelerator, or the thinking making you not want to leave a video game."

"Okay."

"And you, Alyson, are being tricked by your thinking, too. Do you know what you're being tricked by?"

"The thinking behind why I let him off the hook. I know what that is, too. I don't want him to have to suffer. I love him and I don't want him to be in any pain, and I don't want to hurt our relationship."

"It's also an illusion that taking a firm stand is going to hurt your relationship. In fact, in the long run it's really appreciated because it teaches him an important lesson."

They both agreed.

Now both were unstuck. What didn't look possible to either of them when they walked in apparently was possible after all. They thanked me profusely and left feeling satisfied.

When we feel stuck, we're not.

"Stuck" is another illusion. We're only stuck at the level of consciousness we can see at the moment. Why?

Because it's all we can see! Of course we're stuck if it's all we can see. But it's only all we can see because we're looking from a fixed, narrow perspective. We can't see what's at a higher level of consciousness—yet! Whatever is up there brings other possibilities and hope. Our only limitation is what we see with our thinking in the moment.

* * *

Here is another wonderful parenting example excerpted from one of my other books, *Prevention from the Inside-Out* (pp. 257-258). This is Lisa talking:

> The very best thing that Health Realization has done for me is how it changed my relationship with my [seven-year-old] daughter, Bridget. I had my daughter during spring break of my second year of college. She was very sick as an infant. She cried all the time and was inconsolable. It turned out she was allergic to my breast milk, and I breast fed for six months. I remember it was a Wednesday that I stopped breastfeeding and put her on soy formula. Wow! She was a completely different child! That Saturday she cut her first tooth and had her first ear infection. By the time she was one, she had fourteen teeth and twelve ear infections. To say the least, it is very hard to bond with a child who is constantly crying. This continued until she was two. By that time we definitely had issues. She had learned to whine for what she wanted, and I had learned to give her anything just to have a little peace of mind for a moment.
>
> I had talked to Jack many times over the past few years about my relationship with Bridget and how things had to change. I was in a group session with Jack and I was describing my relationship with my daughter to the group.
>
> "She is a manipulative little brat, who does everything she can to make me upset and push my buttons." Pretty much from the time she was born I saw her as a manipulative and conniving little brat.

"Do you think there is any other possible way to think of her, Lisa?" Jack said.

I just looked at him and I was thinking, "Yeah right! I could think of her as an angel, an innocent child who doesn't even know what she's doing." I was picturing this temper tantrum in my head that she always does. I was thinking that I might be able to see her differently, but as soon as I saw the temper tantrum I would continue to see her as manipulating me.

Then something happened! I realized that if I thought of her differently, then the very same temper tantrum would look different!!!! Wow!! The only way I can describe this is like I was wearing a helmet with a red-colored face-shield and someone spun it around and it was, all of a sudden, a blue lens! Everything looked different. I bonded with my daughter that moment, finally! I realized that how I thought of her was what would determine my reality of her!! This was so big!!

My relationship with Bridget did change and has stayed wonderful. I have, for the first time in her life, been able to see the innocence of the sweet wonderful child that she is. (I feel like crying, tears of joy.) She no longer has the temper tantrums. If she does I just don't notice anymore; I see her as tired or having a hard day or needing my attention. Things are so different. She doesn't have to whine anymore or try to get my attention, because when she says, "Mom," I look at her and I listen, instead of thinking that she is just trying to bother me. She has brought me so much joy since then. I can't look at her without smiling at her expressions, or the way she acts, or the things she says. She is my wonderful, beautiful baby girl! If I never get another thing from Health Realization, this was priceless, and I am so very, very grateful.

Because of the way Lisa expressed this I want to make it very clear that we were never talking about Lisa trying to change her thinking about Bridget, and we were never talking about Lisa trying to have positive thoughts about Bridget. It is too hard to substitute one thought for another.

Why? Because the substitute thought still comes from the same level of consciousness, and we're too smart to be tricked like that. Instead, Lisa realized the way she had been seeing Bridget was only at one level of consciousness and she suddenly realized there were tons of other levels through which she could see Bridget. She realized she had been using her power of thought to make up who Bridget was. But was Bridget the manipulative brat she'd made up, or was she someone entirely different? Suddenly a world of new possibilities opened up before her, and it freed Lisa from the prison of how she had been seeing her.

APPENDIX II

Way back when I originally thought of writing the "Pocket Encyclopedia of Parenting" I had developed a list of common problems parents often encounter. The way I suggested dealing with them at the time is no longer relevant because back then I relied on teaching skills and techniques. However, the issues themselves certainly are still relevant. When I saw the list recently it occurred to me that the first step in dealing with any of these issues would be for the parent to reflect on a question, something like: "What is it about this issue that I really care about, and why?" The presenting issue itself is usually not what we are most concerned about; we care most about what is embedded in the issue. So before we confront any of these issues, or when they confront us, it makes sense to reflect on what is really important about these issues to each of us. I would not be so presumptuous to tell any parent what they should care about; I can only speak for myself. *What do I care about and why?* Everybody can ask and reflect on the answers for themselves. Below are my own answers, for myself, for whatever they're worth. [Then, to deal with any of these issues I want to get my feeling right and deeply listen to my children's view of it, preferably before I share my own view. I am open to changing my view if they've got a compelling reason. I certainly want to give the issue some deep reflection before I share my own reasons. We'll consider each issue alphabetically. [Unfortunately, one of the toughest and most complex issues comes first in the order.] This section is not about what to do; it is about how one sees it, which suggests how one then approaches it.

Alcohol and drugs – Primarily I care that they don't harm themselves, and I happen to know more about this than they do at this stage of their lives. I worked in the substance abuse prevention field for many years. Research shows the longer one delays the onset of first use, the less likely the young person will develop a dependency, and if they do they'll be able to kick it easier than the person who starts younger. I know that at each developmental stage they can reckon with this issue at the level they are capable of—the earlier the better. Even **4-7** year olds get exposed to drinking on TV all the time and get the message "drinking is good and the thing to do." So if we see our children watching people drinking on TV at this stage, wisdom might suggest we want simply to introduce an alternative message. If problem drinking has occurred somewhere in our family we might say something like, "Honey, I just want you to know that drinking alcohol is something people in our family haven't been able to handle very well." Or if there is no history of family alcoholism: "When you see people drinking I just want you to know a lot of people get into trouble when they drink alcohol", or, "That's something we don't do in this family." That's it! All we're trying to do at this stage is plant an alternative message to the "do drink" messages they're bombarded by. If they're old enough and curious enough to ask questions we can talk about it. We can ask ourselves, "When they see a do-drink message, what alternative message do I want to occur to them instead?" If problem drinking already occurs in the home it may be a different message: "That's why dad [or mom] acts like ____ sometimes." When children reach ages **8-11** it is especially important to have a discussion because kids are ready to mature in judgment and adult influence is still high. It would be very helpful for kids at this age to learn that during the **12-18** year period much of what our bodies grow into will be determined and all the hormones are in very delicate balance, and to get involved with chemicals during this time can upset the delicate balance we need.

188

When alcohol or other drugs are introduced into an immature system it's like an unstable chair that can be knocked over more easily than a balanced chair (a mature system). With this understanding wisdom might suggest that if kids can make a commitment to themselves at this stage that they don't want to put themselves in jeopardy and therefore they have no intention of drinking or using drugs from now through the teenage years, we're on the right track. But then the true test happens, the moment they are offered their first drink or joint or pill or inhalant. Are they prepared for the moment it will almost inevitably happen? How can I help them be prepared? "Suppose a friend of yours tries to get you to do some drugs or alcohol, what will you do? Don't tell me, show me. I'll play your friend and you try to resist." Then I put on the pressure until the kid gets stuck. At the moment they're stuck we are then primed to have a helpful discussion about what they might do to maintain their integrity and cool at the same time. If this process does not seem to be working, perhaps our kid has already become involved. Once a disease comes along it's too late for an inoculation. But here we can still talk, if the feeling is right. I really want to listen to them deeply here. If a kid is already heavily involved in alcohol or other drug use, talking will likely not get very far, and we may need to get him help. Still, as much as we can we want to keep the dialogue open. Yet we can still say what we will and will not accept for behavior. If it has gotten totally out of hand we may need to consider what Harriet and Emily had to reckon with in the last chapter of this book. [Thank you, Steve Glenn, for much of what is in this section.]

Allowance – I care that they know how to manage money. Which brings up an interesting issue: If what I care about is managing money, do I care how they obtain it? [legally, that is] Should they just receive an allowance simply for being a part of this family? Or should they get an allowance because they work for it? Or should they get a base allowance and if they do extra chores receive an added amount? Any of those is legitimate. If parents believe money should only come through work then the answer would be obvious for those parents. Because what I care about most is that they learn how to manage money, the system by which they get it from me is not of much importance to me. Whichever I choose I just need to be consistent. The other question it raises is should there be any restrictions on how they spend it? Do I care what they do with their own money? Can they buy any clothes they want? Can they use it for tattoos or body piercing? We will deal with that specific issue below, but for now, if we believe any restrictions should exist for how they can use it, those restrictions (and why) have to be stated up front so there will be no confusion after the fact.

Bedtime – I care that they are well rested so they can function well, and so they stay healthy. Selfishly I also care that they're not crabby. If they can do this on their own, great, I never have to say anything. If they can't, I need to take charge because their health is that important to me.

Body piercing and tattoos – I care first about their safety and health. I heard a news report that even surgical instruments in hospitals are not always cleaned properly. Do my kids really know how well piercing and tattooing instruments are sterilized? I am admittedly a little suspicious about it. Secondly, I care that they aren't going to do something later that they will regret, that they can't take back or it would at least be very difficult. Teenagers have a hard time thinking ahead sometimes, and they don't realize the way they see it now can change. Normally I think it is wise to let people learn this type of thing for

190

themselves, but in this case, it might be too hard to take back. On the other hand, it is their own body and they should be able to do what they want with it; or, maybe their body is my responsibility until they're 18. I have to reflect on where I come down about this. Back to the health issue, an alternative practitioner once showed me how metal pierced through the body anywhere on the central meridian (the vertical line all the way up and down the middle of one's body, so you know what areas that covers), or placed on the thumbs or big toes, drains the energy out of the body much like a hole in a water pipe.

Curfew – I don't want to have to worry that they're safe, and if they come home later than agreed to and don't tell me, I know my own thinking would have a tendency to go into worry, and I don't like that feeling. Put simply, I need to know they're all right. I also care about responsibility. If someone agrees to something they either have to stick with it or if something unanticipated comes up I need a call to let me know what is going on. We can deal later on with whether it was an important enough issue to be late for.

Chores – To me, household chores are about responsi-bility; they're about everybody doing their part to keep the household running smoothly so the burden doesn't fall on any one person. But I don't like to see it as a "chore." I see it as an important thing that needs to be done. We could all make a list together of these important things, and make it fun.

Clean room – This can be a tough one to figure out. For me, I care that they are not in unhealthy situation, so "dirty" is more important to me than "messy." However, I care that a messy room does not contribute to the chaotic state of her mind. It's my own deal to like a room that contributes to calmness, but is it important enough for me

191

to put that on my kid? I want to try to help him see the value of it, but how much do I insist upon it, so long as it's not unhealthy? Every parent has to decide that for themselves.

Eating – I care that they grow well and are healthy. If they are not eating it is not healthy. If they are eating too much it is not healthy. If they are eating too many unhealthy foods, it is not healthy. I don't want body image to be such a problem that it affects eating habits. In fact, I have to be a little careful how I deal with this because I don't want the way I deal with it to adversely affect how they see their body image. Despite the way it looks on the outside, body image issues have more to do with lack of feeling well-being on the inside, no matter how one looks. We all have things about our bodies that we do not like or wish were better or different, but those are just thoughts, not to be taken too seriously and it doesn't make sense to allow those kinds of thoughts to override our children's innate well-being. Some people eat to feel comforted, to feel comfort in life, to feel comfort with oneself. Overeating, or eating and purging, or not eating at all, are merely symptoms of not feeling healthy on the inside, and that's what I care about most. Exercise also helps, and that's good for everyone.

Dating – I care that my kids are safe. I care that they're with someone who is going to see the best in them and bring out the best in them, who will treat them with the respect they deserve. I care that my own kids treat their dates with respect and keep them safe. I also care that they are responsible. I don't care who they go out with so long as they are safe, respected and responsible. Of course it would help if I like their date, too, but that's only for my own benefit, so I want to be a little careful with that one.

Driving – This is a safety + responsibility issue. Cars are so dangerous that they have to show me, demonstrate to me that they are responsible before they step foot in one on their own. There is never an excuse to get behind the wheel when one is on alcohol or drugs; there is never an excuse to get into a car being driven by anyone who has had alcohol or drugs. There is never an excuse to text while driving or speed or to be a passenger with a driver who is texting or speeding. Teenagers get into a lot of accidents and I'm not willing to take the chance until I am sure they're responsible. All they have to do is show me by what they do.

Hanging out – I care what they do, not who they see. If they get their kicks out of hanging out with a so-called "bad crowd" they have to realize it may be guilt by association. If they are strong enough within themselves they will not succumb to whatever problematic behaviors that group is engaged in, but it takes an awfully strong kid to resist the temptation when everyone else in the group is doing it. Are they really prepared for that? How will they handle it? Show me—before they're confronted with it. "What will you do if____." This issue is especially where it pays to trade freedom for responsibility. The question comes down to, do I trust my own kid? I want to trust that my kid will make the right decisions but they have to prove to me that I can trust them. I might even give them the benefit of the doubt unless they prove otherwise that they don't deserve the freedom—unless I sense danger, and then it's a no-brainer; then I'm not willing to take the chance. But otherwise, "If you demonstrate responsible behavior you can have all the freedom you want (after a certain age.)"

Homework – I care that my child understands that working at something produces results. I care that they understand there are certain obligations and responsibilities that occur anywhere in life. In school, these obligations have to do with following school rules and doing homework. Personally, I am not fond of schools overloading kids at home with an overabundance of homework, but that is not in my control. It doesn't give kids the right not to do it just because they don't like it. The more wise effort that gets put into homework should be reflected in the results they get. What I'm after is seeing improvement, commitment to doing well, commitment to putting one's best foot forward, because I know they will benefit from that for the rest of their lives—not the content but the practice. So what does this mean when things interfere with homework, such as video games, texting, Facebook or whatever the next electronic fad is? If I see my kid neglecting her work because of those things she is not going to be able to do those things until her commitments are honored. If I see that my kid manages to get his work done but it's always very stressful because he's spending so much of his energy on screens, to me that's almost as harmful as not getting it done at all. So in that case it's freedom for responsibility again. If he can't show that he's responsible about this he won't be able to do those things until his obligations are met. If he shows he's responsible, he can be trusted to get done whatever he needs to whenever he wants. It's up to him.

Ignoring – Why would a kid ignore me or his mother? I want to step back, observe and listen. Does he say he's going to do something and then doesn't do it? Or, do we direct her to do something and we're lucky if we get a grunt? What's behind whichever it is? Is he so zoned out in front of a screen that what we say doesn't even register? Have we been nagging so much she doesn't even hear us anymore? Depending on the answers to questions like that will determine the direction we want to go with it. To me, however, ignoring is often a respect issue. Is ignoring someone showing them respect? I don't think so.

Morning; getting out in the morning – I care that I'm not late for my own obligations; that wouldn't be responsible of me. I also want a nice start to my day. I don't like to start my day filled with stress, anxiety and frustration. I want it calm. So I may not be willing to be late, but at what expense? I don't want to have to jump all over them, to nag at them to be ready, to be on their case. So, calmly, we're going to discuss all the things that need to get done by a certain time, and I'll help them know what to do and help them as much as I can. I'm going to give them ample time to be ready and I even may want to remind them a couple of times, but I also want them to know that when I have to leave they're going to be taken out in whatever state they're in, ready or not. If they're still in their pajamas, that's their embarrassment, not mine. But I can't do it out of anger or frustration; I need to do it calmly, without fanfare. "I'm sorry, sweetie, it's time to go now." If they don't like that feeling, they'll be more sure to be ready the next time. If they whine or yell and scream about it, that's not my problem. It would be wise of me to tip off the school or day care to let them know what I'll be doing.

Out of control – I care that they know how to calm down. If they don't know I have to teach them what calm is, why it's important, how they know when they have it, what gets in its way, how they can find it if they lose it. I don't want to teach this when they're not calm because at that time they will not be able to hear me.

Peer pressure – I care that they know that no one from the outside can make anyone else do anything; it always comes from the inside. Even if someone holds a gun to your head, you still make the internal decision to comply or risk being killed. That's still up to you. It's always up to you. I care that my kids know how to listen to their wisdom and that they actually listen to it. [Beyond that, it's the same as what I stated in the paragraph on "hanging out," above and in "smoking," below.]

Procrastination – Procrastination usually ends up equaling stress. I don't think stress is healthy. Therefore procrastination isn't particularly healthy. Procrastination is about putting things off that have to be done and that ultimately are going to be done anyway. I want to help my kids see the value of not putting something off, how much better it makes everyone feel, especially the kid herself.

Sex – Sex is about so many different issues. To some parents sex is a moral issue and I totally respect that. It is a safety issue; it could mean disease or with HIV/AIDS it could even mean death. It is a not-doing-something-you'll-regret-later issue. Sex is not something one can be too cavalier about because one little mistake one little time could mean pregnancy, and being forced to make a horrible decision between having a baby way before one is ready, or carrying it to term and having the baby adopted, or being faced with an abortion, none of which are good options. Therefore it is also a responsibility issue. It is also a respect issue: I care if my son or daughter is going to be intimate with someone, that they are totally respected by (and respect) the other person. Here is another area where I know more than they do. I know that sex is a lot more than just a physical act. Suppose the two people have different expectations: what if for the girl it's about love and for the boy it's about getting as much sex as possible (or vice versa)? If there's imbalance like that, is sexual activity right? Suppose the other person would just tell you what you want to hear so they can conquer you? How would you know? Sex is also an emotional issue. I know many young people are not emotionally ready to handle all the emotions involved. In other words, having sex is possibly the most complex of all issues, and simply wanting to do it because it feels good or because you like the person does not consider all the complexity. There are so many potential ramifications; it is not something to take lightly or casually. Some parents insist on abstinence, and that's okay; the question is, what will work best? I don't really want my kids to have sex before they are mature enough because I'm not sure they understand all these ramifications. But I also don't want to be overprotective. Primarily, with the issue of sex I really want their own wisdom to prevail (which, of course, includes safe sex).

Sexting, or putting naked pictures of oneself over the Internet – I care that my child does not do something that s/he is going to regret for possibly the rest of her or his life. I care that they have the common sense and wisdom to not get involved with these kinds of things because they always have a way of coming back to haunt you. I care that they have the respect enough for themselves and their bodies where they wouldn't put themselves in that kind of position. I have seen kids share pictures that were meant only to be shared with a friend and had it end up all over the Internet for everyone to see. Again, because I want wisdom and common sense to prevail, it would be wise to have a caring, nonthreatening discussion about these issues.

Smoking – I care about their health. Smoking, first and foremost, is a safety issue. I know kids typically smoke to show they're cool. I also know addiction is not very cool. Kids can be helped to know how to very coolly refuse something they don't want to do by turning the tables on those who offer. "No thank you. I would never do that to my body. I care about myself too much." If they call the kid a chicken or a wuss or whatever name they come up with, the kid can calmly and coolly say, "Hey, you can call me whatever you want. It doesn't bother me. You can do whatever you want. It's not going to change what I care about." If the kid is already smoking they just don't understand enough about their own health and well-being or they don't care (right now, that is, later when trying to kick the habit because they're really sick, believe me, they'll care. But by then it's too late.) Teenagers and preteens feel indestructible. It's my job to do my best to help them see otherwise and to help them know how to engage their own wisdom about it.

Sibling rivalry – Sibling rivalry, like whining [see below], is primarily an "attention" issue. The idea is to get the parents' attention, and for some strange reason most kids would rather have unpleasant attention than no attention. If they are seeking attention by fighting with their siblings, wisdom would say I don't want to reinforce it by giving them attention at those times. All I want them to know is, "I'm sure you can work it out together." On the other hand I want to be sure I'm giving them enough good attention at other times when they've done nothing in particular to deserve it, just because they're my children and I love them. If one child is substantially bigger than the other and someone could get hurt, then it also becomes a safety issue and that's where I have to draw the line and remove them from each other. But I would want to do that with as little attention as possible. "If you can't play together without being safe, then you can't be together now." Period. But, ironically, I know siblings who fought like cats and dogs when they were younger who now are a lot closer than siblings who hardly ever fought. So who knows?

Temper tantrums – The issue with kids who have temper tantrums is primarily that they have learned that's how they get what they want. I want to reverse it. They are out of control and I need to help them understand calm and how to find it.

Whining – [See sibling rivalry above.] I just don't like to hear it. That and temper tantrums are not how I want my kid to learn s/he can get things from me. Sorry, it won't work, is the message. Then I have to steel myself and let it run its course until the kid realizes it's not going to work anymore, and it will die down on its own over time. That's what wisdom tells me. But I really can't give in to it. I have to know the whining will first escalate before it peaks and eventually goes down. I have to know that's going to happen and be prepared to ride it out all the way, no matter how loud and annoying it gets.

There are many more issues of course. If you don't see your particular issue on this list, you can still ask the same questions and step back, listen and observe and let wisdom call the shots.

References and Bibliography

Glenn, H.S. (1988). *Raising Self-Reliant Children In a Self-Indulgent World*. Rocklin, CA: Prima Publishing.

Mills, R.C. (1995). Health Realization Parent Manual. Alhambra, CA: California School of Professional Psychology. To inquire about possible availability, contact Center for Sustainable Change, Gilroy, CA. at: info@principlespsychology.org

Mills, R.C. et al. *Informed Families* Parenting Series (videotape series). Probably out of print but to inquire about possible availability, contact Center for Sustainable Change, Gilroy, CA. info@principlespsychology.org

Pransky, G. (1990). *The Commonsense Parenting Series* (audiotape series). Possibly still available from Pransky & Associates. mail@pranskyandassociates.com

Pransky J. (2011). *Modello: A Story of Hope for the Inner-City and Beyond.* British Columbia, CA: CCB Publishing.

Pransky, J. (2003). *Prevention from the inside-out.* Bloomington, IN: AuthorHouse (888-519-5121).

Pransky, J, (1991). *Prevention: The Critical Need.* Bloomington, IN: AuthorHouse (888-519-5121).

Pransky J. (2011). *Somebody Should Have Told Us!: (Simple Truths for Living Well).* British Columbia, CA: CCB Publishing.

Stewart, D. and Stewart, C. (undated). Can Love Survive Commitment? (audio tape). Unavailable (to my knowledge).

Other Recommended Readings

- Banks, S. (1998). *The Missing Link*. Renton, WA: Lone Pine Publishing
- Banks, S. (2001). *The enlightened gardener*. Renton, WA: Lone Pine Publishing
- Banks, S. (2007). *The enlightened gardener revisited.* Renton, WA: Lone Pine Publishing
- Chen Mills-Naim, A. (2010). *The spark inside. A special book for youth.* Gilroy, CA: Center for Sustainable Change, Gilroy, CA. [a book for teenagers] info@principlespsychology.org
- Pransky, G.S. (1990). *The relationship handbook.* [Blue Ridge Summit, PA: Tab Books]. LaConner, WA: Pransky & Assts. mail@pranskyandassociates.com
- Pransky, J. & Kahofer, A. (2011). *What is a thought (A thought is a lot).* San Jose, CA: Social Thinking Publishing. [a picture book for little children]
- Stewart, D.L. (1993). *Creating the teachable moment.* Blue Ridge Summit, PA: Tab Books. (out of print – may be able to find it on ebay or half.com)

About the Author

Jack Pransky, Ph.D. is Director of the *Center for Inside-Out Understanding* and is an international consultant and trainer for the prevention of problem behaviors and the promotion of well-being. He also authored the books, *Somebody Should Have Told Us!*; *Modello: A Story of Hope for the Inner-City and Beyond*; *Prevention from the Inside-Out, Prevention: The Critical Need* and co-authored both the *Healthy Thinking, Feeling, Doing--from the Inside-Out* curriculum and guide for middle school students and *What Is A Thought (A Thought Is A Lot)*, a picture book for little children. Pransky has worked in the field of prevention since 1968 in a wide variety of capacities. He has offered parenting training and consultation to a great number of parents, and has trained many parenting course instructors.

CPSIA information can be obtained at www.ICGtesting.com
Printed in the USA
BVOW02s1355121114

374734BV00001BA/151/P

9 781927 360644